JACK JOHNSON

AND HIS TIMES

Jack Johnson
and his Times

by Denzil Batchelor

Weidenfeld and Nicolson
London

Picture acknowledgements

The photographs in this book are reproduced by permission of the following:

Barrets 5 (below); *Boxing News* 1; *Hulton Deutsch Collection* 4 (below);
Ron Olver; 2, 3, 4 (above), 5 (above), 6, 7; *Planet* 8

First published 1956

This paperback edition published by
George Weidenfeld & Nicolson Limited 1990

Foreword © Harry Carpenter 1990

ISBN 0 297 81037 5

Printed and bound in Great Britain by Guernsey Press Co. Ltd., Guernsey C.I.

To
Learie Constantine
who never drew the colour bar against me

Foreword by Harry Carpenter

Only thirty years ago I saw blacks being directed to the back of the bus in the USA; in Galveston, Texas, as a matter of fact. But American sport had long since cast apartheid away and in boxing black champions generally have been accepted and admired by white people since the 1930s. Joe Louis saw to that.

The life of Jack Johnson is a chilling reminder of how different it all was in the early days of this century. He came from Galveston and as I once wrote in a book of my own, 'To be black in those days and also a good enough fighter to whip white men was practically unforgivable. To be black and be the best fighter alive was unthinkable.'

Johnson was certainly that. There can be few people alive who saw him fight, but what film remains portrays a sleek-limbed, smiling athlete confident of his own ability, whose style was notable for an arrogant casualness, hands held low, feet set firm, until a sudden change of pace, a canny sidestep, and a blur of hands betrayed the danger that was in him. He also had a sly tongue which he used to taunt opponents. In pursuit of the title he was forced to chase Tommy Burns halfway round the world, catching up with him in Sydney, Australia, and subjecting Burns to humiliating defeat.

As if this lazy black power was not enough to sour the blood of every redneck American, Johnson also had the effrontery to consort with white women. These sexual adventures led him into conflict with the laws of his land and turned him into an outlaw.

If a rebel such as Johnson existed in today's world of boxing he would be as famous as Mike Tyson and his liking for flashy cars, big cigars and champagne would endear him to the media, let alone his talent for thumping out jazz on a 7 ft bass fiddle.

In the years I followed Muhammad Ali around the world I saw in him a resurrection of Johnson. Here was another extravagantly gifted black boxer with a mind of his own and a way with words. He, too, fell foul of white authority and was hounded out of boxing at the peak of his powers. But times had changed and white fans everywhere admired Ali. They hated Johnson. Even when he lost his title they accused him of throwing the fight.

I

◆◆◆

THE JANITOR'S BOY was the easiest target in the school. He was a tall, slim Negro and looked strong enough, but you could always mock him to your heart's content and be sure that he would never dare answer you back with his fists—unless perhaps his sister Lucy was around. The reason the boys mocked him was that as soon as school was over, instead of beating it to the swimming pool, the janitor's boy had to put on an apron and sweep out the school buildings to help his father. There was a good reason for this. His father was a sick man. Long ago he'd been a knuckle-fighter with a punch in both fists, but now that he was a pretty old man he was semi-paralysed. The reason for this was that he'd suffered terrible privations when fighting in the Civil War under General Lee. More than once in the campaign he'd gone for days without food or water.

He was a stern man, the janitor. He insisted that his boy went to school every day, even when the sun made the island of Galveston off the coast of Texas so blazing hot that the rich white folk who managed the cotton warehouses and the port in the Bay called it Devil's Island. No slipping away to the beach for the boy! All the fourth grade claimed that they had heard howls for mercy from the janitor's house, though whether it was the janitor or the janitor's wife who tanned the hide off him for wagging it from school, no one could be quite certain.

One thing was certain, however. It was the janitor who made him sweep up as soon as school was out, and that was when the boy's life was most like hell, because the rest of the fourth grade would forego even a swim to glue their noses to the window and shout insults through the glass.

The other children seemed less sensitive than the boy in the janitor's apron. The other boy, Charley, was a good scrapper, though his eyes were bad. The three sisters were nice girls, though Lucy was a tough lady. She was always goading John Arthur—such was the name of the boy the fourth grade made its butt—to fight his way to public favour. She urged him to avenge every insult with his fists. Sometimes he would try, but he generally got beaten. That was where his mother came in. If John Arthur came home the worse for

9

wear, she'd give it him again, hot and strong. She was a midget of a Negress—everyone called her Tiny—but she had an indomitable spirit. Years later John Arthur remembered the way she treated him as a kid; and years later Tiny Johnson remembered too. 'Jack was a rank coward as a boy,' she said, 'and simply would not fight. He was eternally getting into trouble with his playmates, and he always got the worst of it. His sister was his chum, and she had to do all the fighting. I hadn't time to be bothered settling children's fights, and I told Jack that if he got licked again I would give him another whipping, because he was getting old enough to defend himself. Sure enough he got whipped by a smaller boy, and I gave him a hiding when he came home; but I never had reason to whip him again. He developed confidence and muscle. . . . He always said he would reach the top of the boxer's prize list. He was no better nor worse than the average boy, but he's a good son, and provides well for me and his sisters and brothers.'

When life was peaceful it was a happy enough existence for the janitor's boy. Galveston was a happy-go-lucky town, and reasonably prosperous. The twenty-eight-miles-long island, up to a couple of miles wide, boasted in those days that it was the second port in the States (only New York City was ahead of it), and the biggest of all in the Gulf, with New Orleans a respectful second. The cotton-seed refineries were working at full pressure; the flour and lumber mills were doing a thriving business; so were the shipyards and the breweries. There was no reason why, when John Arthur had worked his way through grade school, he shouldn't get a pretty fair sort of job; especially as everyone had to admit he was an intelligent sort of boy, even if a bit on the cowardly side.

But the boy wasn't satisfied. Even the evenings on the beach, strumming a guitar to the light of the moon on the silver Texan bay, weren't enough to satisfy him.

There was a legend in the family that he was cut out for the larger life. An old Negress named Dinah who lived down the road had called in to see Tiny a few days after he was born, had looked at the wrinkled baby palm and impressively announced, 'Dis chile am going to eat his bread in many countries.' No one in a poor Negro family in the South could have such a prophecy uttered about him without feeling that he was marked out for a special destiny.

One night he decided that he couldn't bear it any longer; the sternness of his father, the scoldings of his mother, the sneers and insults of the other boys and the fights which he never seemed to win. The moon was on the Bay. You could see carts crossing to the mainland by the road bridge and the plume of smoke from one of the railway bridges where a train was carrying its passengers to New Orleans or perhaps even to New York. It was a great wide world and no one had to be a slave in it. He whispered, 'Good-bye, mammy,' as he climbed out of his attic window and slid down the pipe to the ground. He'd a dollar or two in his pocket, and he was strong and could work. Though he was only twelve he looked older. By morning he was riding the rods north. The first great adventure in the epic life of John Arthur (better known as Jack) Johnson had begun.

It was a hard life, but he stuck to it. More often than not the only food he tasted in a day was the crust he could beg. Sometimes he went without food at all. Well, if his father could starve while Lee's army fought at Atlanta and formed the rearguard in the famous March to the Sea, Jack would show he was a man of the same mettle. The best chance of a job, of course, was in a racing stable. He was light enough to ride exercise, and he had a way with horses; and if you fitted in a trainer was liable to take you on, and no questions asked. He moved from one stable to another, and after several hungry years had passed he got himself employed at a Boston stable run by a Mr Moore who later became a Senator. So far he owed life nothing. The number of square meals he ate in a week was less than a horse in training. He was homesick for his mammy; and it could be cold in Boston. It would be nice to go back home, but though he'd jumped the rattler on every train from the south he was scared to take a return ticket by the same route and he wasn't earning enough money to pay his fare.

But there was a hope. Joe Walcott and Scaldy Bill Quinn were in town, training for their fight at Woburn. One or other of them might want a sparring partner. He tried Scaldy Bill first, and begged his hardest.

'You get to hell out of this camp before I throw you out on your face!' was Scaldy Bill's answer. Jack Johnson left with the tears streaming down his cheeks; frustrated, miserable, humiliated.

But at Walcott's camp he met a different reception. Mrs Walcott saw him first.

'Say, you look hungry,' she said before he had had time to explain his hopes and ambitions. If it came to that, he hadn't any ambition then much higher than the plate of pork chops she set before him. He'd just cleaned up the fat with the last crust of bread when

Walcott came in. Johnson stood up and Walcott's practised eye took him in from wide shoulders to the feet protruding through his boots.

'How old are you, son?'

'Seventeen.'

It was true. Five eternal years had passed since he slid out of that attic window.

'You're big—over six feet. What do you weigh?'

'Around hundred and fifty, sir.'

Walcott laughed. 'You need more pork chops,' he said kindly. 'You want to come help me out? All right, you come. Ever had any experience of this sort of thing?'

'None.'

'Doesn't matter. You'll get it. There always has to be a first time. Come and put the gloves on.' He added: 'Sonny, it's a great game if you don't forget to pull in your chin.'

It was wonderful! He didn't give him a broom and tell him to sweep out the changing-room. It had taken five years to do it, but he had got himself promoted from janitor's boy at last.

The first time, as it turned out, wasn't as easy as all that. He sparred with Walcott on Revere Beach, and Walcott saw no reason to pull his punches. The great little Negro's jabs went into Jack's ribs like bullets and jerked back Jack's head till it wobbled on the stalk of his neck. But Jack had the pork chops inside him and a glimpse of a wider world to inspire him with hope and confidence. What were the fierce thrusts of Walcott's fists compared with the thrust of the long steel rods of the railway guards striving to get rid of any starveling Negro boy who might try to ride the rattler from New Orleans up to the North? He took the punches and came back smiling for more. He was a hardier, braver boy than the kid who had slunk out of Galveston five years before.

Besides, Walcott, though he said nothing, understood the sort of material he had added to his camp followers. He himself had run away from home before he was old enough to shave, to ship as cabin boy from Barbados to that very Boston where he had found the down-and-out Johnson. He had fought his first fights for $2.50 purses, and, if it came to that, six long years were to roll before he was to fight (and roll on the canvas) against Rube Ferns for the distinction of calling himself the best welterweight in the wide world.

Even so, Joe Walcott, with his long arms and teak-tough body, was one of the great men of the ring and perhaps as good as he was going to be when he became a champion. The fact that this kid from Galveston (wherever that might be) was prepared to come into the ring and paste him all over the head and body, not caring what he got back in exchange, appealed to the Barbados Demon.

He told Howie Hodgins, his manager, that he wanted Johnson in his corner when he fought Scaldy Bill Quinn; and this decision was one of the wisest he ever made in his life. Jack did not want Walcott to beat Quinn: he wanted him to kill him. He had not forgotten how Scaldy Bill had met him when he was broke and starving, and wanted a job above everything else on earth.

This was a side to Johnson that had to be appreciated if you wanted to understand his character in the ring. He was thrusting and fierce when he was was fighting, but he was vicious to the last drop of blood in his body when he was feuding. Hurt his pride, make him your enemy, and he wouldn't be content with just beating you in the ring. He would humiliate you before the world, and then chop you into little pieces. In the years to come many men were to learn this truth; Frank Childs, who denied him a bed on the floor on a Chicago winter's night; Tommy Burns who told him he was yellow; Jim Jeffries who drew the colour line, and hated and despised Negroes. On the night of the fight between Walcott and Scaldy Bill Quinn he had to smash down the man he hated vicariously. He did his best to make a job of it.

After seven rounds Walcott—leading on points by a mile—turned to him and asked how he was doing.

Johnson pulled a grave face. 'You're not doing bad, but you're not doing so good. Breaking even maybe. You ought to carry the fight to him a bit more to be sure of it, if it comes to a verdict.'

After that Walcott nearly fought himself to a standstill, battering away at the hulk that was Scaldy Bill Quinn. In the seventeenth round he dropped him for good, a senseless lump reddening the canvas. That suited Johnson. He gazed at the bloody hulk with the satisfaction of a pilgrim who has kept his vow.

After the fight the press swarmed into Walcott's quarters. They promised him he wouldn't have to wait long: he'd soon have Tommy Ryan off his throne—or Mysterious Billy Smith, if he happened to have deposed him first. Walcott laughed. He hadn't many illusions about his worth.

'So you think I'm on the way to be champion of the world, gents? Well, maybe you're right, at that. But I want you to know there's another world champion right here in my camp. A boy who'd never had the gloves on till he sparred with me at Revere Beach. A kid in his teens. His name's John Arthur Johnson.' The reporters were interested. Most of them wrote the name down in their note-books, some of them putting it in their columns next day. But those who wanted to see John Arthur Johnson were disappointed. He'd been paid off and reckoned his services were no longer wanted, so he'd slung his hook. He'd slung his hook because Galveston was calling. The sough of the sea at night; the tinkle of banjos all around the bay. The taste of fried chicken, and the cool bliss of water-melon on a broiling midsummer day. He'd slung his hook for a glimpse of his mammy again—her hair would be greyer now and her little face skinnier, but her voice would be the same as ever; her low, happy laugh as merry as when he was a piccaninny.

He'd done his job, earned his little roll of dollars—now he was going south! Once on the way he strayed off, because he had the ambition to pick up a few nice pieces of money, to buy a great big viol, bigger than anyone had seen in the State of Texas and just the thing to give as a present to his mammy. He got the job at the racing stable easily enough. Anyone could see he knew plenty about horses. He could handle a horse with the temper of an octopus as coolly as anyone, and though he was really too heavy for any but the top weights he could ride exercise well enough.

But one day as he was doing out the stable of the shortest-tempered brute on the strength, he got a kick on the leg that snapped the bone the way a match-stick is snapped between a man's fingers. He lay on the stone floor and hoped the horse wouldn't kick his brains out, and just before the horse could carry out this plan his master arrived and dragged him head first to safety. And then poor Jack broke down and blubbered.

'Oh, sir, if only I could get home, home to my family—home to see my old parents before they die.'

He decided to include his father. It cost nothing extra and maybe the boss would think twice as well of him for being a loyal son in both directions.

The boss was moved. A friend of his had told him the night before a long rigmarole of a story to prove that if it was lucky to kill a China-man it was twice as lucky to help a broken-down nigger. The boss dug into his pocket and gave the kid the price of freedom.

Back from the north to Galveston! He thought about the road back. Through the trim New England farms and the tobacco plan-tations of Virginia and the endless cotton-fields of Carolina and

Alabama, through the tall forests of Georgia, past Vicksburg in Mississippi where his father had fought with Lee, through the swamps of Louisiana, where the tree-frogs croaked while the huge moon swung in the blue velvet sky—to the wide horizons of Texas at last. The oil fields and the cotton fields, the peacock-coloured sea glimpsed all the way from beyond Baton Rouge to the first sight of the shining island on the horizon that was Galveston itself.

But as a matter of fact it wasn't to be that sort of home-coming at all. They shipped him on board a boat, and when they were almost home told him that there was smallpox aboard, and he was in quarantine. He was skinny enough to squeeze through the porthole and wade to shore.

Home at last! The return of the outcast at seventeen, no richer, no poorer than the child of twelve who had vanished into the night, but at least with the biggest viol ever seen in the State as a home-coming gift for his mammy.

She didn't burst into tears when she saw him. She didn't cast forth trembling arms to embrace him. She had one good look as he came up the road, made sure it was he, and turned her back on him to stump into the kitchen to make a pot of coffee. That evening she upbraided him fiercely for breaking all their hearts and wouldn't look at the outsize viol whatever he said. A week passed before she stopped on the veranda steps and listened to him playing 'Swing low, sweet chariot' and he knew he was forgiven.

The next thing was to get a job. There were no horses to curry-comb in Texas; there was no Joe Walcott to spar with on the Harbour Beach. He tried his hand at various things, amongst them the job of waiting in the big hotels on the mainland. It wasn't bad, because you could listen to the orchestra playing the new tunes from Europe, the songs Yvette Guilbert was singing as she drew her long black gloves over her skinny fingers in the music halls of the Latin Quarter.

> *L'homme est une bête féroce*
> *Qui ne songe qu'à son bonheur*
> *La nuit après les noces*
> *Il vous perce le coeur . . .*

And then parties from New Orleans would roar with laughter at the next line, and the manager would pounce out from behind a pillar and fine Jack twenty-five cents for not attending to his job.

Except when this was happening it wasn't bad work in its way, but not peaceful enough. After a while he found a better job in Dallas—working in a paint shop. It was a nice quiet occupation, and you never got fined for anything, and messing about with paint appealed to the child in the heart of the Negro.

In the paint shop there was a youngster named Wally Lewis. He was a well-built fellow and he liked to box. Whenever there wasn't much work on hand and the foreman was out of sight Wally Lewis and Jack would spar a few rounds. The young fellows in Dallas who had time to stand and stare said this Johnson kid was quite a boxer.

When he was nineteen Jack went home from the mainland for a holiday. At the same time that he arrived in Galveston a boxer named Bob Tomlinson came to town with the circus. Jack was interested in him. Bob's line was to give a show inside a booth, challenging anyone present to stand up with him for four rounds. If you were still on your feet at the end of the fourth you collected five dollars—big money in the Johnson household. Jack paid his dime several times to watch Tomlinson in action and came to the conclusion that he would not only stand up with him: he believed he could beat him.

At last the time came when he felt he should try. Tomlinson took him lightly—perhaps there were Galveston boys in the booth who told him that they remembered this kid a few years back when he was the coward of the fourth grade, if not of the whole school. Tomlinson began as if he had only a few seconds' work ahead of him, and for three rounds he called the tune. Nevertheless knocking the Johnson kid out wasn't quite as easy as the local know-alls had promised. The kid knew how to clinch. He clinched so good and hard you might have thought Joe Walcott had taught him. Then in the fourth round, when Tomlinson's—or at least the management's —five dollars were at stake, the kid came to life. He landed a couple of pile-drivers on Tomlinson's jaw, and the boxer reeled and sagged. His manager quickly rang the bell to save his man. Jack was five dollars richer, and that night the Johnson family had fried chicken for dinner.

After the victory over Tomlinson, the future was more clearly defined. Jack decided that being a painter was less of a vocation than he had supposed. He would be a boxer instead. He had the punch; he had the speed; he was capable of moving half a second before trouble arrived in his neck of the woods. The boy the school had jeered at was the hardest nut to crack in all Galveston. Why, the very next day he heard them talking about him at the street corner. Harry the Carter reckoned he was better value than the Bearded Lady. Old Matthew, who had seen Peter Jackson before the English turned him into a spoiled darling, said that one of these days Jack would be almost as famous as Peter—but everyone reckoned old Matthew was an awful liar and in no way worth listening to anyhow.

The main thing was that the Sporting Club and the stag parties and the little showmen who put on Battle Royals immediately sat up and took notice of him. This suited Jack. It was no hardship to him to be one of six Negroes pitchforked into the ring, last man left standing to collect the purse of five dollars. His sleek panther's slide out of trouble, his quick pounce to hammer a man temporarily off balance—these won him many a Battle Royal. And when all five of the others turned against him as soon as the fighting started, he would always find a way to turn them against each other, even if it meant taunting them with his tongue.

Soon enough he was booked up for his first real professional contests. The record books do not unfold the full story of these engagements. In some places you will read that Johnson's first fight was against Jim McCormick, otherwise known as the Galveston Giant, with whom he is reported to have boxed a seven-round draw on 11 February 1899. Elsewhere the first full-scale professional engagement is said to be the ten-round bout with Sid Smith, in which Jack was given the decision. Anyway, by the end of 1899 he had been blooded in the ring. He was a boxer with a record.

Only—where were his opponents? They weren't to be found in Galveston. The promoters liked him; were all too willing to give him a good place in their programmes, but the opposition by no means queued up to give him his chance. Quite often he was glad to earn five bucks for an exhibition contest. Not infrequently he rode the rods out of town in his painter's overalls—for he found himself obliged to go back to his old job to earn enough to keep himself fed— to town on the mainland, where he had persuaded promoters to give him a chance on the bottom of the bill.

It wasn't any fun riding the rods. The railway guards would rout about under the coaches with long, steel rods, in search of human game. If they could roll a nigger under the coach wheels that was a good deed for the day. Johnson's defence was too shrewd for them, however. If they spotted him lying on top of a coach, a gang of them would chase him down the train, shouting threats and abuse which probably made him love white men no more than he instinc-tively did already. But he was always too quick for them. He was always sure-footed enough to escape from coach to coach, and cun-ning enough to take cover somewhere so that he slid off safely when his station was reached. Then he was ready to fight six or ten rounds for fewer dollars, and take the night train back home—without the formality of a ticket.

By the end of the century he had earned himself a few dollars and a home-town reputation, but that was all. No one except Joe Wal-cott—and he had lost touch with him—would have been such a fool as to suggest that the underfed kid from Texas was going to be the champion fighter of the twentieth century.

II

◆◆◆

IT WAS A BROILING DAY. He'd swept up the paint shop early. No one was going shopping on such a blood-warming afternoon. No one was going to do anything but sit in the shade with his toes off the burning street and eat water melon if the water-melon boy could be induced to cross the road to sell a slice for a cent.

But the street wasn't cool enough for Jack. 'Hey, Ambrose,' he grunted to the kid next door, 'somebody's been sitting here already and hotted it up for me.' He spat the big, shining black seeds lazily at his toes—those seeds might be cool. 'What about the sea?'

'Bones says someone's swam in it and warmed it up too.'

'I don't care, no-how. I'm going swimming.'

'When?'

'Soon. Soon as I get up.'

'That ain't soon.'

'Wha' dyuh bet?'

'Bet you a million.'

'Bet you two cents.' Ambrose, the realist, coveted water-melon and recognized that the boy would want a hundred per cent tip to cross the road with his tray.

'You come too.'

'All right. Why not?'

The two boys lay gasping like stranded porpoises in the steaming street. Neither made a move.

'Ever knew it so hot as this?' asked Jack. Ambrose didn't answer. His mouth was too hot to talk.

Jack sighed. Even on the hottest day there was always a breeze from the sea in Galveston. If you lay at a street corner you would be cool before evening, though once in a while you had first to whip some kid who thought he'd got a right to your favourite pitch. To-day there wasn't a flutter at the cross-roads.

What was more the sky was queer. Jack reflected that it was the sort of sky his dad had told him about that time he'd been in an earthquake. 'A sky you couldn't see,' his dad had said. It was queer why you couldn't see it. There was a sort of curtain of gauze drawn over it, a curtain of a billion specks of dust. His dad had supposed each speck had been a bit of a home or somebody's child or a pineapple plantation a few hours back, and now they all blew across the sky and put the sun out, as you might say.

The gauze curtain hung over the world. Jack was scared, so scared he jumped to his feet. 'Come on, Ambrose. Let's get to the sea.' When you were in the sea, you were away from it all somehow. Streets and people and cotton fields and oil refineries could blow up on you. You'd only to duck your head and slide down into that cool green world for a few seconds, and you were saved. When you came up the city might be blown off the face of the earth, but the sea would be the same, the same great green waves, the same singing silence, the peace that had been there before they had built the city.

Ambrose took the water melon boy's cycle, and the boy was too hot to throw him a curse. Jack went into his house and routed out his machine from the room where his mother sat sewing.

'Come *on*, Ambrose. Race you to the beach.'

'You couldn't race a scabby tortoise.'

But neither of them was to reach the beach. As they free-wheeled downhill they noticed that on every side men and women were clambering to their feet, beginning to shuffle into the roadway, starting to run uphill to the top of the town, downhill to the sea. Their faces were staring and terrible, like the faces of people with a curse on them. Their lips never moved, their eyes did not blink. You could see the nameless horror that possessed them in the flare of their nostrils, the shining stare, the glaze of their eyes in the red twilight. A man pulled at Jack's bicycle, and Jack kicked his blank terrified face till he let go and fell in the street to be trampled by the soundless throng shuffling uphill.

Then, suddenly, above the thrum of feet, a shriek like the scream of a woman who sees her child being murdered. The crowd swayed, turned back to look, and began to wail and shriek too. For a moment they stood there, screaming and sobbing, yet not knowing what fear was clawing at their hearts. Then, in an instant, swift as a thunderbolt, the invisible fear became clear and tangible. The molten sky was riven. The caged wind came out like the souls of the dead bursting out of hell itself. It screamed and galloped across the sky. It seemed to hit the far curve of space and cannon back, roaring in torment. It went racking round the roof of the world belching and bawling.

Then it dropped like a black bolt of lightning on to the earth itself. It hit the earth howling and flung itself off up the hill, hurling over trees and people and houses as it came. Jack took its blow in the face, and felt his cycle bend under him like rubber. The next thing he knew was that he was on the ground. He saw the legs of the world surging forward upon him; legs in trousers and boots, bare legs, the thin shaking legs of children, lovely legs of women, for which men would have given their souls yesterday. Legs were his enemies. He crouched against them, slashing out with his fists at them, butting them with his bloody head. He tore at skirts and tattered trousers and heaved himself to his feet. Above the crowd's head he saw a window frame flying towards the sea. At the street corner the hurricane slashed down a swathe of men and women like a wheat field in a storm. He saw a child's body blown like a little black foot-ball down the street to smash against the sea-wall.

He was screaming, yelling at the top of his voice, yet he couldn't hear himself at all. He twisted his neck and tried to find Ambrose in that seething mob, but he couldn't see Ambrose anywhere. Never again was he to see Ambrose, and no one was ever to hear of Ambrose any more. Ambrose was become an anonymous red smear on the road, or perhaps a hank of hair picked up long afterwards among the pebbles on the seashore.

The crowd was pounding down Market Street. You couldn't hear their wailing now; only the thunder of feet. What was more, you didn't dare look up to the sky. Down at the bottom of the street, where the bridge joined the island to the mainland, a dreadful sight greeted Jack's eyes as he pulled himself up in the face of the advancing crowd. The purpling sky lowered down and the iron-grey sea rose up.

He saw the sea stand up. It was a miracle, but he saw it. The sea reared up like a lion; and, roaring like all the beasts in the world, sprang over the city in a great pounce. He heard the thundering wave, he saw the sky crack open and the cliff of rain crash down, engulfing the earth. You couldn't hear anyone cry out now. You could see faces twisted into masks of terror, mouths widening, tongues protruding, eyeballs goggling. But there was only the deafening thunder of endless sea flying overhead like a colossal bird clapping wings of iron half the size of the sky.

Jack flung his arms round the woman in front of him. As the wave fell upon them, the children clutching at her skirt were whirled away from her and sped out of sight, sucked down in that tumultuous river like twigs in a millrace. He saw an old man rise above the flood, shout up his thanks to Jesus his Saviour and vanish under the crest of a wave high as a house before the words were out of his lips. He found himself kicking to keep afloat, kicking against faces and bodies, kicking against the cattle that went past brandishing their horns for an instant before they were sucked down in the tug of the tide.

At the road's edge a tree-top reared, and he plunged for it with both hands. He felt his ribs crash against the boughs, as if gigantic gloves were hammering his body. But his hands gripped; he held on. He swung his legs up. He was saved—if the tree didn't snap in the pulverizing force of the flood. From where he crouched he saw the water rush by below, with the bodies of men and cattle borne along as the torrent sprang back to the heaving ocean. Here and there cresting the waves went the wall of a house: overhead in the furious wind a corrugated iron roof-top skimmed the water like a flat pebble which you use for skipping stones.

The sea was flooding home now. Down below the bodies lay in drifts, like spindrift when the tide drags out. He saw a big bearded man wading, chest deep in the water, tugging at the dead bodies, searching among the drowned for the wife he had clutched to safety a moment ago.

Jack sat in his tree-top for a while, then slithered down to earth. Somewhere above Market Street, among the floods of the higher part of the town, his family were trapped in their little house. He plunged and swam and fought his way through the seething water; he waded, and struck up the hill. The great wave had engulfed all Galveston. In the narrow streets above the harbour the water was still deep as a lake, the bodies were still thick in its swirling eddies.

He found his home at last. On a flat roof above the water a score of poor Negroes were huddled hopelessly together. In the dim light you could read the despair in their blank faces. They were too terrified to weep or shriek; they huddled together like little black cattle on the threshold of the slaughterhouse. As he plunged towards them a second wave came thunderously through the streets, strewing the dead on either side of the narrow road.

Under the flat roof was Harry the Carter with his cart and pair of horses. He was standing up in his driving seat and brandishing his whip towards the streets at the top of the hill. 'Here you are, folks,' he cupped his hand to shout, 'just a dollar. Only a dollar a time up the hill to safety!'

For a moment, before the last lights of the city blinked out to leave the stricken world blanketed in darkness, Jack saw the despairing faces of his family and friends who hadn't a cent to save themselves and those they loved. For a moment he saw Harry's crowing face—the face of a hopeless, hard-working man who sees in a moment of tragedy the chance of wealth he has been waiting for all his life. Then he flung himself through the waist-deep water at the carter and struck the words from his mouth with the first blow of the fight.

Harry reeled round to face him. 'Why, you scum, you. Steal my horses from me, would you, you filthy scum!' He struck out with his whip, determined that no one else was going to snatch his racket from him. Jack closed with him and the two went down together under the hooves of the rearing horses, under the water, among the drowned cats and chickens and the flotsam of chairs and tables. When they came up they could hardly find each other in the dark, but at last they came to grips and punched and wrestled till Jack landed a punch that sent the carter under water with his horses floundering on top of him.

The big carter scrambled up. Jack picked him out, a shadow against the darkling water. He hit out—and it wasn't Harry at all. Then he heard his man surging through the water towards him. He saw the glint of his white teeth in a snarl like a death's head. '*Give you half, Jack.* Split it with you.' He hit into the white, snarling teeth.

Harry closed with him; his long fingers wound round his throat. Jack brought his knee up, the way the bad boys in the gym would bring their knees up in the corner where the referee couldn't see. Harry bent over, spewing, and Jack uppercut him out of the waves. The two men tore at each other with their bare hands.

'Half is yours, Jack. Half is yours.'

Jack hit him with a right cross. Harry half sank in the water, his hands groping forward. A great rabbit punch burst like a bomb on his neck. He struggled to bring Jack down as he fell.

Jack was on his feet. He wasted a moment or two attempting to find the fallen man and grind him under heel. Then he turned to the roof top.

'To the top of the hill—and safety—free for all!'

They took a long while to realize it. Old Jacob Briant, who kept the tobacco shop next door but one, began to shout: 'I haven't no dollar, Jack, but you can trust me. I used to trust you for candy when you were little.' Then, slowly, the truth got through to them, and they began to help each other off the roof. Mrs Jarrett, who took in washing, and the very old body who was doing fine sewing till her grandson was through college (no one ever saw him again), and old Bessie Maley, and the young woman called Della, who every-one said was no better than she should be, and Mr Walker, the minister, they all sat on each other's knees in Harry's cart. There were Tommy and Liza Broomhill and their Aunt Patsy and Patsy's dog Mobsman, and a little bantam cock that belonged to the Broom-hill boy, who might be alive somehow at his cousin's house half-way down the hill.

And of course the Johnson family were there. The old man was there—Jack had to hoist him to safety through the deep water; the legs that had got rheumatic fever from the long days of battle and privation under Lee couldn't carry him across the street now.

Jack's mother was the only calm person in the cart-load. She sat on one of the minister's knees and the harlot Della sat on the other, and they sang hymns all the way up the hillside to safety. Charley and Jack's two sisters squeezed in beside Jack on the driver's seat. By the time the cart got to the Mission House on the top of the hill, everyone on board was singing '*All God's Chillun got Wings*' in voices fit to melt the heart of Simon Legree. 'You sing real pretty, chile,' Tiny Johnson told Della.

The old minister came out to greet them. 'Thank God, here's somebody alive. Come along in—come along in. There's coffee, boilin' hot. There's cakes and sausages. Come in, all you good folks.'

Jack was out of the driver's seat and gripping the minister by the arm. 'My mother,' he said, 'she's poorly. Coughing terrible before the water hit us. Get her to the hospital, that's all I'm asking you.'

The minister put his arm over his shoulder. 'My son, the hos-pital's gone. Gone into the sea. The great wave broke it up and bore it away. They're all dead and drowned, the good doctor and all.'

He walked through the town as if there never had been a tidal wave or a hurricane. Ambrose, he thought, I'll never see Ambrose again. He owed me four bits from the pinochle game. I liked Am-brose. I liked the water-melon kid too.

They'd found the water-melon kid. He was one of the 5,000 drowned in Galveston that night. Fishermen had hauled him in, one of a hundred bodies the tide had knotted together in a huge heap, rolling it through the waves like seaweed in the bay where the oil-tankers lay. A hundred human beings. Fighters whom Jack had known in the Battle Royal and little kids who hadn't learned to read yet, and women for whose bodies the men strutting on what was left of Market Street would have given plenty—all their limbs tangled and twisted together like strands of seaweed in the sluggish, heaving tide.

No one could tell who was dead, and who would come back to-morrow. Mammy Laxton sat in her doorway with a mad woman's smile on her ancient face and sang a song she made up as she went along.

> My boy's coming home to-morrow,
> There'll be no more pain and sorrow,
> We'll go to Jesus together,
> When it's sunshiny, summer weather.

The children gathered round her door and watched her, their mouths round with wonder. At last one or two began to giggle, and she beamed back at them and asked them inside and gave them milk and honey cakes. Mr Walker, the minister, came to see her and read to her about the New Jerusalem that was all gold and jewels and psalms rising like incense, and told her to go on her knees and give thanks that that was where her boy was.

And just as she was kneeling, the door opened and her boy came in, the way she had always said he would. He couldn't tell where he'd been, or what he'd seen, or what he'd done or how he'd come back. His mouth gaped and his eyes stared, and while Mr Walker and Mammy Laxton sat on their hunkers and spread up their palms and sang 'hallelujahs' till the road filled up with staring children, the son stood in the living room with hands drooping like a zombie and staring empty face.

But as the minister and the mammy sang, from the town below came the wailing of women; the widows, the bereft mothers, the women wailing for their dead. The keening hung on the air like smoke. The weather was blue and beaming now, summer weather from everlasting to everlasting. Only, throughout the dazzling days you heard the wailing of the women by the harbour, from the highest streets above the town.

And if you stood in the brilliant noon to look down on Galveston, you saw the smoke rising in a pillar, all over the town. The funeral pyres were burning, as the women wailed for their dead who might be among those smouldering heaps, or among the mighty piles of corpses packed in the deep trenches, or in the stuffed holds of fishing boats going out to give the sea the dead that the sea had claimed—the blue and beaming sea that looked as if it could never hurt anyone.

All day long and all night long, for days and nights on end, the weeping of the women could be heard through the town. At last, one night, the last pillar of smoke ascended and died away. The last boat came silently back to port, to take on a new cargo again— the old cargo of cotton which had made the town prosperous in years gone by. And above the thin sound of weeping a banjo could be heard in a downtown street; a banjo playing, and the sound of dancers shuffling through the measures that had brought delight to the young men and maidens before the tidal wave and the hurricane brought a city down as Troy and Nineveh had been crushed and left desolate in the old time before history began.

III

✦✦✦

AFTER THE GALVESTON DISASTER, Jack soon found his first fame as a fighter. His success against Jim McCormick, whom he regularly met at this time whenever spending money was short, and his good showing against Klondike in Chicago, persuaded the Galveston promoters to arrange a fight of major importance for him in his home town. The chosen adversary was Joe Choynski, known to an earlier age as the best heavyweight who never won the title.

Joe, a Jew with a Greek god's appearance, was thirty-two when he fought Johnson, and had all his famous fights behind him. His most famous of all was his battle with Jim Corbett on the barge near Benicia, California, in 1889. This was a grudge fight, if ever there was one. It was, in fact, rather too much of a grudge fight even for the Californian authorities to swallow at the turn of the century. The original intention was to smuggle the two men together into a barn ('somewhere in the country' was the most exact description Corbett would give of it) where the contest was to take place as soon as all the supporters had been relieved of their guns. The two men battled for six ferocious rounds, during which Jim annoyingly knocked his right thumb out of joint by punching Joe on the jaw, before the sheriff clawed his way up into the loft where the contest was on view and apologetically stopped the fun. He had hoped that he would arrive too late, but as it was if the boys would go over into the next county, the sheriff would be grateful and take no action. When they accommodatingly went down to the station, however, they found half San Francisco ahead of them and no hope of getting aboard the train.

Jim and Joe were annoyed at such invidious attentions. Since articles were signed, two detectives had hounded them out of town and over the countryside. On one occasion the two pugs had to beat it disguised as a society couple in the MacAllister equipage behind a pair of spanking trotters belonging to a leader of the *haut monde*. It really seemed as if their best efforts to have a perfectly peaceful battle to the death, or the nearest thing to it, were being deliberately persecuted.

However, love (and the fight game) will find a way; and in the

end a barge was rented in the middle of the Bay off the small town of
Benicia. On board the ring was pitched; the crowd—a hundred
strong—were occupying every inch of space not needed for the
contest, indeed five of them had already fallen into the bay and barely
escaped drowning. But nobody cared what happened to mere spectators. The serious thing was that Joe Choynski had lost the five-
ounce gloves with which he had begun the battle in the barn; it was
generally believed that one of Joe's supporters, figuring he was
essentially a bare-knuckle man, had considerately dropped his gloves
overboard. Now the rules—in so far as this strange promotion had
any rules—provided that the bout should be concluded with the
same pair of gloves with which it was begun. Corbett, however,
mindful of his injured hand, consented to continuing in his five-
ounce mufflers, while Choynski was armed with the skin-tight
driving gloves offered by a business man standing at the ringside.

The great fight—and it was one of the hardest struggles in history
—was begun at noon, and every round was fought out under a
tropical sun. Corbett vowed that 'a sturdier, tougher fellow than
Choynski never stepped into a ring', and he was certainly a better
man when he fought Gentleman Jim than when he tackled Johnson.
The battle on the barge was so close that Harry, one of Corbett's
brothers, could no longer bear to watch it, and was discovered by
another brother, Frank, weeping with his head over the gunwale.
It appeared, on his own admission, that he couldn't bear to sit
around and watch Jim get a licking—a pusillanimous attitude which
Frank quickly corrected by hitting Harry on the nose and challenging
him to a supporting bout outside the ropes.

But for Jim it was a devilish close-run thing, all the same. He had
to clinch like a Cumberland wrestler in the fifteenth round, and in
the next session saved his energy by stalling in the one small plot of
shadow cast on the floor of the ring from the look-out house on the
little deck above.

At last, in the twenty-eighth round, Corbett's tactical training
brought him victory. He swung his injured right fist in a series of
haymakers which were meant to miss; but Choynski used up so
much energy in evading them that he slowed down until he became
all but a stationary target, and Corbett was able to land one final
left-hand punch that toppled him over for good—if it hadn't, the
winner declared that he himself had been perfectly ready to drop
dead.

A sturdy, tough fighter, Joe Choynski. None on the Pacific coast, whence he came and where he had most of his early contests, could be called his master. He went to England in 1892, and won three fights as easily as kiss-your-hand. He knocked out Jim Hall in 1896, beat Ed Smith on a foul in the following year; and six months later—fifty pounds the lighter man—held James J. Jeffries (in two years' time to be champion of the world) to a draw after twenty splendidly contested rounds. In 1898 came a draw with Tom Sharkey (who knocked out Choynski) a couple of years later in Chicago. The fact that Choynski was beaten in 1900 by Joe Walcott in New York should by no means be regarded as a blot on the escutcheon. It is true that Choynski was ten inches the taller and forty pounds the heavier man, but the fact was that a week before the match he had fallen in the street in Chicago and broken a rib. His engagement in New York was to meet not Walcott, but Kid McCoy. He had asked to be released from the contest, but was held to his bond, although McCoy was allowed to withdraw, having acquired Walcott as a substitute.

Altogether it can be seen that by the time Johnson got his chance against Choynski in 1901, the coming man was meeting a fighter with a historic reputation, even though it was assumed that he was a little past his best. Moreover, Choynski was not by any means on the slide. Even after he had fought Johnson in 1901, he was good enough to outpoint Frank Childs and knock out Peter Maher.

The bout with Choynski in Galveston was certainly the first big chance in Johnson's life. If he won it, the way lay open to the top of the tree; if only he could persuade Jeffries or Corbett to withdraw the colour bar and meet him on level terms.

As it happened this was a worry that lay a long way ahead for Johnson. The contest with Choynski showed all Jack's promise, but underlined his inexperience. His footwork was admired by the *cognoscenti*; his defensive skill made old men bore their juniors with reminiscence of little Charley Mitchell of England—'Jolly Cholly'—who sometimes had to run and hide, because he wasn't always big enough to fight.

The fight lasted just three rounds. In the third round Joe landed a left hook to the temple (a punch which Benny Leonard was later to regard as his private property), and Jack crashed over on his back. He declared in later years that this was the hardest punch he ever received in his ring career. Johnson was struggling on the floor of the ring, though according to Choynski he was utterly incapable of beating the count, when five giants in ten-gallon hats sprang into the ring. Each whipped out an outsize pistol and levelled it at the referee or one of the fighters, and the leader of the raiding party cupped his hands to bellow above the din that he was the head of the Texas Rangers and had come at the request of the Governor to arrest the principals in the fight. Before he had finished speaking, the sheriff and his deputies appeared with more pistols and more ten-gallon hats.

The boxers were led off amidst sympathetic cheers and impounded in the local prison. There they stayed for twenty-eight days, after which it was held that there was no case against them and they were dismissed. On Johnson, at least, the little episode left no scars. In prison you were sure of regular meals, with pie on Sunday, and no one could make you work until you had got yourself convicted. In later life, Johnson was to run round the world to avoid the stigma of prison which he considered was enough to break his old mother's heart. History does not record whether Mrs Johnson's heart was less fragile in her younger days, or whether a month in prison as an unconvicted suspect didn't count. All that is known is that Jack was gently tolerant of the law's intervention on this occasion. One old man who was present at the ringside held the view that this was because he had some fear of beating the count, in which case the arrival of the Texas Rangers saved him from worse punishment than he received in prison.

One thing is certain: the enforced rest was good for Jack in the development of his career. The world noticed him for the first time; the world began to talk about him. In prison with Joe Choynski—that was a real achievement! You got much more attention from the world for being 'in' with Joe than for being out and about, defeating all comers.

What is more, as soon as Joe came out, the world took the trouble to ask the old warhorse all about the dust-up down in Galveston. As Johnson had only lasted three rounds most people believed that he must have been a push-over. Joe soon disillusioned them.

'They told me Johnson was a novice when they asked me down to Galveston to fight him. He's no novice. The novices are the experts that didn't recognize that this boy is a coming champion.'

The boxing writers began to wonder where they had heard the name Jack Johnson before, and one or two of them with long memories recalled what Joe Walcott had said about his sparring partner.

Meanwhile when Jack came out to face the world, he did not find a long queue of Texan boxers anxious to exchange compliments. The boys who had not yet fought Johnson congratulated themselves on their luck and swore that it was never going to get any worse, if they had any say in the matter. One trick in particular which the new-comer to the top rank seemed to have picked up in this fight they were particularly anxious to avoid: the little habit of parrying a blow by landing heavily on his opponent's biceps. It looked painful, and Choynski was said to have admitted that it *was* painful: moreover, that he had not come across such a habit before in all his seventeen years in the ring: not against Fitz, or George Godfrey, or Tom Sharkey, or Peter Maher, or Corbett, or Jeffries. The big boys in Galveston shook Jack's hand warmly when he came out of the local prison; and then said good-bye.

To earn a living, he had to leave home once again. The best bet seemed to be Chicago. 'That's right, boy, you go to Chi. They'll all want to see you in Chi,' said Jim McCormick after he had fought Jack for the fourth time in four months and didn't want to see him again for four years at least.

It was true that Chicago was the headquarters of the game at that time. You'd find such boys as Jack Root, Peter Maher, Billy Stiff, Frank Childs, Marvin Hart and Tom Sharkey making big money in Chicago. If you were big and clever, it should surely be possible to earn a good living in Chicago.

And yet when Jack arrived there, he found it as hard to make a living in Chicago as in Galveston. Perhaps he was too big and too clever. Anyway, the important fighters steered clear of him for a while. The best he could find were a few club performers, like himself desperately anxious to get engagements for grub stakes. He knocked out a number of these, though the contests do not appear in the record book.

He counted himself lucky when he got a job as sparring partner with Jack Root, the Austrian-born boxer who in the following year was knocked out by George Gardner in the first contest for the world's cruiserweight title. But he didn't hold that job long. Root's manager complained to the boxing writer who introduced Johnson to his camp that what he had asked for was a sparring partner, not a champion. It was very nice to know that such compliments were being bandied about his name, but it would have been even nicer to have stayed on as Root's sparring partner and been sure of room and board.

He was out on the street. He hadn't money and he hadn't a roof to sleep under. Chicago can be very cold in the winter; and the snow lay in the streets in February 1902. Jack had spent the few dollars he had earned for the six round draw with Frank Childs, and he would have frozen to death in the gutter if he hadn't run into Childs himself.

'How's things, Jack?'

Jack shuddered. 'Things is as cold as they can be.'

Frank Childs laughed. 'Only old Klondike can fight in the cold,' he said. He looked pitying at Jack. There wasn't much going on in Chi if you were a Negro boy.

'When did you eat last, fella?'

'Lunch time, of course.'

He hadn't said which day. Never mind. You didn't ask. The dead-beats had their code.

'Would you care to share my room? It's too big for me any-way.'

'Well, I might,' said Jack, who would have shared a kennel with a police dog. 'Whereabouts is this wonderful room of yours?'

'Just up the block. There's a big stove in the middle of the room. I ain't got no second bed, but there's a mattress. You could put it right beside the stove.'

The snow fell, flake on murderous flake. The two men from the South sauntered along, with all the dignity of the human race, to the room up the block with the big stove in it.

'This way,' said Frank Childs. It was a very wonderful room. There was a bed in it. That was, of course, for Haroun al Raschid, Frank Childs himself. There was a chair, in case Frank Childs got tired of lying on the bed and sought a change of attitude. But most marvellous of all, there was a stove. 'It glowed like a big red apple,' Jack used to say, remembering the welcome gleam at the end of years of good living.

'Make yourself at home, boy,' said Frank Childs. 'It's all yours. Except the bed and the chair, of course.'

All Jack wanted was to be near the stove. There were a couple of blankets he could put on the floor right beside the stove and curl up for the best night he ever had in his life. In the morning, or around about mid-day when even a Negro has a right to be awake in a snow-storm, Frank Childs dug out sausages and coffee from a drawer in the corner of the room. Plenty of sausages and a great big pot of coffee. You didn't only keep warm and sleep in this paradise, you ate and drank too. Frank Childs was the most wonderful benefactor in a wonderful world; and some day the snow would stop and Jack would find himself a job as a sparring partner.

But the snow didn't stop. It was still falling ceaselessly on the fifth night that Jack curled up beside the glowing stove that had become his best friend on earth. He had gone early to bed when the door opened and Frank Childs came into the room. At his heels was a huge Negro, big enough to eat a boxer at a meal.

Frank Childs shook the sleeping Johnson. 'Wake up, Jack! Wake up, brother—and get up.'

Jack stirred uneasily, and sat up. 'What is it, Frank?'

'It's the end of your little stay with me, boy. My cousin from Memphis is in town. He's sharing the room with me. Get up—I say —get up, and get out!'

Johnson prayed and begged and wept and pleaded. Through the uncurtained window he could see the perpetual snowfall against the night, beautiful as an ermine cloak and sure death to a penniless Negro. He begged in vain. Frank Childs wouldn't let him huddle down in the furthest corner of the room. Family obligations were sacred; his cousin from Memphis must be entertained to the limits of his powers.

Out into the frozen world stumbled Jack Johnson. Years afterwards, telling the story to Nat Fleischer who relates it so vividly in his biography of the champion, Jack would recall the wind that greeted him as Frank Childs slammed the door behind him. It was as sharp as a dagger and cut you to the bone.

He stumbled along Michigan Avenue, his hands digging deep into his pockets. And there, in the lining of his pocket was a coin: a genuine, God-given, miraculous nickel! No coin that ever saved a life was more gratefully seized upon. No one who had tramped Michigan Avenue with an empty belly in the savage winter of 1902, could doubt what use it should be put to. There, on the street corner, was a saloon which had the hospitable habit of offering a free counter-supper to its customers. All you had to do to be eligible for a plate of liver and onions was to buy a glass of beer for a nickel. Jack put down his last coin in the world, and ate what he had reason to suppose might be his last meal. And somehow that meal made a new man of him. It gave him strength to brave the snowstorm and the blank future; and courage to face a world which was darker than the Chicago night.

And, as it happened—as it so often happens—revenge was just

around the corner. Johnson won a few minimus fights in the Middle West, decided that the area was not one in which he could expect to prosper, and lit out for the Californian coast. In Los Angeles, in glorious midsummer weather when a man feels at his best, a friend who was running a promotion asked Jack whether he would like to have a fight in the programme. The time had not yet come when Jack could turn down any such offer; but when he heard that his opponent was to be Frank Childs from Chicago his enthusiasm knew no bounds. 'Would I fight him?' he exclaimed. 'Would a guy want a warm bed on a cruel cold night?'

Johnson spared Childs nothing of the grudge he bore him. Four times in his life he was to bring to a fight something more than the mere determination to win. He brought a murderous hatred into the ring against Burns, who taunted him with cowardice while fleeing him across the world; against Jeffries, Negro-baiter and Negro-hater; against Ketchel who double-crossed him; and against Frank Childs, who had the inhumanity to turn him into the night when he was frozen, starving and friendless. For the first time in his life Jack Johnson fought a man in the ring with more than his fists. He fought with his heart—and with his tongue. He told his tough opponent just what was in store for him, as soon as he met him in the ring; and during the contest as Childs reeled before him he did not hesitate to rub in the moral. He hit him with a left jab for the loss of the blankets; with a right cross for refusing him a place on the floor on that January night nine months before; with the one-two for depriving him of the stove that had glowed like a big red apple—and with the bone-crushing right uppercut to remember him to his family. As he was to toy with Burns and Jeffries, so on that glorious night in Los Angeles he toyed with Frank Childs who was good enough even at thirty-five to beat almost any man in the game and who had actually beaten Walcott a fortnight before.

The victory forwarded Johnson's career, but it did more than that. It taught Jack how good he could be when his heart was in a fight. He was only twenty-four and still far from developed physically— not yet a fully-grown heavyweight. But he told himself now that the time was coming when he would be able to meet the biggest men in the world on level terms.

The penniless years, the icy years, had held few consolations. The week you'd been in work, as a sparring partner or on the winning end in a prelim at the Star Theatre on Chicago's North Side, there had been some pretty good parties, but never as merry as those Jack found in California in the endless sunshine of 1902. There the boys and girls gathered together and ate fried chicken and drank beer—you didn't need champagne. There was dancing, not, it was true, to the music of an orchestra in monkey suits, but to Chatty Bill's concertina and Little Murder's mouth-organ. The ballroom wasn't any swank honky-tonk on Nob Hill, but Jacob Bowie's bedroom in Niggertown. There all the artless bliss that Negroes can bring to the mere act of living was given full rein. And there one night Jack met Sadie.

There had been women in his life before: not a few, if fewer than there were to be in Harry Greb's—he liked to sleep with a girl in his dressing-room immediately before pulling on his trunks for the ring. There'd been girls for Jack in Texas and in the North. You didn't win fights without getting some offers. Some of the nicest girls he'd known had been as simple and innocent about wanting him for a lover as children asking for chocolate cake at a Christmas party. But Sadie was different. Sadie didn't want Jack just to sleep with, as a natural act to fill in the long, panic-stricken hours of the dark. She wanted to own him and not be owned by him, to be loved by him and hated by him, to shape his mind and un-shape his soul. He knew the first time he ever saw her that she was going to get her lean brown hands on his life and twist it into knots.

He asked Jacob Bowie who she was.

'Her name's Sadie.'

It wasn't, but Jack always spoke of her by this name in later life, when the chapter was ended. In the circumstances, it was a good idea.

'Take care, Jack,' said Jacob. 'She ain't at liberty. She's going with the big guy.' There was a giant from the shipyard, merrily drunk by the window, who generally pinched her behind as she two-stepped past him.

'She belongs with me.'

'O.K., Jack. Don't say I didn't tell you.'

She left the dance and came over to him. 'Where do you live, Jack?' Somehow she'd found out his name! He felt as happy as when he'd won his first fight.

He told her where he lived. He was doing fairly well then and on his way to bigger things. He'd got a good-sized apartment with a swell bed in it: he only wished he'd made that bed in the last couple of days.

'O.K., Jack, let's go.'

He found himself saying: 'What about your chap?'

'Oh, someone always puts drunks to bed. You never heard of a drunk come to any harm. Besides—he isn't my chap any more. You're my chap now.'

When they got to his room she didn't say anything about the bed. He needn't have worried. The door wasn't even shut behind him when she pulled him down on to the bed, on to the rumpled sheets and the mattress showing where the thin blanket didn't quite stretch across. And from that moment the bed was the bed of a sultan, or an emperor. There wasn't just one girl in it, but every woman in the world. There was a whimpering virgin and a harlot with a face of granite, and a devil who knew more about the joys of hell than you could bear to learn. And in the morning when he came back from the drug-store with the two-for-a-dime cigars, Sadie had made the bed and cleaned up that one-room *seraglio* so that it was fit for the parish priest to visit for breakfast.

He'd made seventy dollars that week, and owed nothing. He'd made up his mind to send his mother twenty bucks; she could get a fancy box of the chocolate creams she enjoyed so much and a peacock blue dress, or something. Instead, he spent the twenty bucks on a brooch in a shop window Sadie said she liked. That was how fond he was of Sadie.

How fond Sadie was of him was something he could never be sure of. There was the time when he swore he saw her drinking beer with the big fellow from the shipyard on a night when she was supposed to be visiting her sick mother. By the time he'd forced his way through the smoky saloon she was gone, and none of the people sitting around her table would admit that there'd been a girl there at all.

When he tackled her about it that night, she said with a wooden face. 'That's right, I was there. And I brought my mother too. Didn't you see her? She was sitting right there at the table with me, with another fellow.'

He had been dumb enough to say: 'I thought your mother was supposed to be sick.'

'She isn't *supposed* to be sick any more. She died to-night.'

It was true. But whether Sadie had been at the death bed, he couldn't be sure.

And now times were getting better. Sadie had stuck with him when he was fighting for what he now thought of as pork and beans. She had been his inspiration and his reward. It had appealed to the melodramatic, romantic streak in him to dedicate his opponents to Sadie. As times got better, these human sacrifices got better too. Jack had gone to California in search of white game on the hoof and the blood lust in Sadie's heart was satisfied when she saw the big fighters Jack slew to her honour and glory. Not enough of them, it was true, were white. Boxers drew the colour-line against Johnson as quickly as a Texas Ranger could draw a six-shooter. But there was the massive Klondike to flatten in thirteen rounds; and of course Frank Childs again, and even bigger game among his fellow Negroes. There was the vitally important victory over one white: Jack Jeffries, brother of the great boiler-maker, for so long champion of the world. There was Joe Kennedy, twice a victim. Best of all was George Gardner.

When he was through with the fight game, Jack chuckled as he remembered that the fight with Gardner might be claimed to have won him his first world's title, for Gardner was boss (or nearabouts) of the cruiser-weight division, and the contest was billed as for the Championship. It didn't matter much in those days. Nobody cared very much who ruled the roost among the light heavyweights and Jack certainly never went to town to claim this empty honour. As far as he was concerned George Gardner was just one more victim to be offered up on the altar of Sadie.

Johnson beat George Gardner on points over twenty rounds. Gardner was Irish born: he came from Lisdoonvarna, County Clare. He was almost six feet in height and just inside the light-heavy-weight limit. When he fought Johnson he was twenty-five years old, tough and clever, lathy in build and with a reach only a little shorter than Sam Langford's. He had beaten Frank Craig, the Coffee Cooler, in England, and had won and lost to Joe Walcott and Jack Root. He did not pack a prodigious punch but his feet skipped like the little hills in the Psalms, and that long left hand of his poked out at the most inconvenient angle and with the speed of a humming bird in its dart for a midge.

The fight was the most important Jack had had yet. He was becoming known at last. Since he had come to the Pacific Coast the terrible days of obscurity had melted like the Chicago snow. He had beaten half a dozen first-class men and fought two terrific drawn engagements with the gigantic Hank Griffin whom in later years he described as the hardest or second hardest hitter he ever met in the ring. He was twenty-four, and on the way up. If he could beat

Gardner he would have established his right to a place in the sun. The best men in the game would not look down their noses and pretend he did not exist any more.

In a way, it was a pity he had to take his career seriously at this time. It was more fun to sit under a striped umbrella with Sadie beside him and a glass of cool beer on the table and watch the Pacific roll sleepily in to crash in snowy foam on the foreshore of the Golden Gate. It was more fun dancing till the first rays of the warm sun silvered the black water of the bay and then go home to a forenoon of bed—and Sadie. But he knew then, as he admitted afterwards, that this fight with Gardner was the turning point in his career.

He set about training in earnest for his date with destiny; and then disaster struck him down. Nine days before the fight, as he left the ring after his morning work-out, he suddenly staggered and put out his hand for the support of his trainer's arm.

'What the hell's up, Jack?'

'For God's sake, a bowl—quick!'

It didn't come in time. He vomited over the floor of the gymnasium. He shook his head wearily, drew a couple of heavy breaths and tried to stand up. His trainer caught him just in time as he reeled and fell forward.

'What you been doing, Jack? You been breaking training when I'm not there to watch. You been on the booze, you louse.'

But he hadn't. And the longest night in Californian history in Sadie's arms couldn't explain the jag of pain in his stomach, the sick dizziness that clouded his brain.

His trainer and sparring partner humped him over to a couch. Somebody ran for a doctor.

'You must keep him quiet. He must go to bed for two, three days. At the end of a week he'll be up and about again, probably.'

The trainer sniffed. 'And what happens about his fight?'

'He's lost his fight already. His temperature's one hundred and two.'

Jack stirred on his couch. 'I'm fighting nine days from now,' he said. He knew that if he didn't go into the ring with Gardner in nine days' time he might not corner him again in nine years. This was his chance and he must take it—half-dead or alive.

And in nine days' time he fought George Gardner, the best man in the world at his weight. All he had swallowed in those nine days had been water biscuits and milk and soda. His stomach was still veined with pain and when he stood up the world swam before his eyes. But he was there in the dressing-room on time, ready for the chance of a lifetime.

The worst was yet to come. As he reached the ringside he looked up and the lights hurt him like a punch on the eyes. Then he prepared to slip through the ropes and a jab of pain seared him under the ribs. He felt as if he couldn't straighten up, as if he must fall on to his face. Then some instinct made him reach for his toes, and as he bent he rubbed the pain downwards from his groin with his right palm. He remained ludicrously bent for a long moment while the crowd began to laugh and whistle. Then he straightened up. Miracle of miracles—the pain was gone! He felt light as a bubble in the air; but he felt suddenly marvellously strong. Health seemed to flood his veins as pain and misery had clogged them before. He slipped through the ropes and danced like a happy dervish in his own corner.

All the same, he was weak. He couldn't help but be weak. Biscuits and watered milk add power to no man's punch. As Gardner came from his corner and spiked him with that long teasing left, he wondered whether he had the stamina left to last out the night. The thought of Sadie at the ringside stiffened his back, put weight and power into his clenched fists. He had dedicated George Gardner to her—the victim could not escape his sacred destiny. His fists flew home. Afterwards Gardner told Jack Root that from the first round he had the feeling that he would as soon tangle with a buzz-saw.

This tribute from Gardner was remarkable because Johnson himself always considered that he won this particular bout milling on the retreat. Gardner led repeatedly, but especially in the early rounds while he was still testing his stamina, Johnson was content to slip the attack and counter-punch. Before the fight was halfway through he had established a handsome lead on points and was in a position to chase his man without fear of reprisals.

In the twelfth round he came close to knocking the lean fellow out. Gardner threw a colossal right-hand punch, which Johnson neatly evaded; as he slipped the blow, he came in himself with a right-hand jab over the heart that all but dropped Gardner in his tracks. A couple of days of solid diet in place of those emasculating slops, and that would have been the end of the fight. As it was, Gardner survived, to be made into a chopping block in the nineteenth and twentieth rounds. There could be no doubt as to where the verdict would go and Gardner remarked afterwards that he reckoned himself to be in luck to finish with a head on his shoulders, adding that from then on his money was going on Johnson whoever was in the other corner.

IV

◆◆

FOR A YEAR OR SO there was plenty of easy money to be picked up backing Johnson against all comers. There was Fred Russell, the first of several good men to be beaten in Los Angeles: he was followed by Denver Ed Martin and Sam McVey. There came a little trip away from the Coast, paid for over and over again with the purses won from defeating the big white boxer, Sandy Ferguson, in Boston, and Joe Butler in Philadelphia. Then back to the Coast for engagements with this new fellow Sam McVey and Sandy Ferguson once again.

The money was pouring in: and pouring out. Sadie had a fur coat said to be ermine and certainly just as good. Sadie had an emerald ring and a necklace as blood-red as a necklace of real rubies. The apartment was no longer a one-room affair, but a good-sized place with a white marble bathroom and orange silk curtains. There was talk of Sadie having a lady's maid, but Jack was so enthusiastic for this project that she thought better of it.

And then, out of a sky as clear as a Californian dawn, the bolt fell. Jack had been away at Colma, beating the daylights out of Sandy Ferguson in twenty rounds: a routine engagement but bitter hard work none the less. When he saw the necklace of lights round the harbour and knew he was home again he felt a lightness of spirit he hadn't felt since he saw Frank Childs swallow his punches. It was late as all hell, but Sadie'd be waiting for him in the silver sequin dress he loved and there'd be champagne in the ice-box. He was home and hungry, and in love: one day he'd be champion of the world. He went up the stairs singing 'The Girl in the Golden Brocade'. It was *his* tune—his and Sadie's. Just for singing it he'd earn himself a better kiss than many a man got on his honeymoon. He put his key soundlessly into the lock: he'd tiptoe in and surprise her.

He tiptoed in right enough, but it was not Sadie who got the surprise.

He knew instantly that the apartment was not merely empty, but dead. Nobody lived there any more. He went into the bedroom. The door of the cupboard which had contained the coat that was believed to be ermine, swung idly in the breeze from the window. He couldn't see into the cupboard but he knew the coat wasn't there. The emerald ring wasn't on the dressing-table, the necklace had gone, the silver-backed brushes had flitted. Back in the sitting-room he found a drawer of his desk prised open and not a green-back left among all the rolls of notes that he kept there.

But that was nothing. A burglar could have done that. The horror wasn't that everything was gone, but that Sadie was gone too. There was no lingering fragrance to remind you of her by her dressing-table; there wasn't a crumpled cushion on the drawing-room settee. She was gone. She had quitted his life as if she had never touched it at all. There wasn't anything left of her, not even the novel by Ouida she put aside on the bed last night for more interesting business, with the corner of one page turned down to mark her place.

In the bedroom he found a note from her on the floor, under the chest of drawers. No doubt she had left it on the dressing-table in the conventional manner, but the breeze through the open window had carried it away. As he scrabbled for it on the floor he was aware how ridiculous she was making him look, now at the last—or beyond the last. . . .

The note told him all he needed to know in half a dozen stark sentences. It was, of course, as he had known ever since he saw the swinging door of the empty cupboard and the bare dressing-table, Barty who had taken her from him. Barty was a racehorse trainer, a high yellow with the tongue of a college man who'd been everywhere and seen everything; though you couldn't help but feel, not from the front row.

'Where've you been all my life—at least since I got out of prison the last time?' he'd asked Sadie when they met at a supper at a Nob Hill party. It had passed as witty.

He was patronizing to Jack. 'Where I come from they're asking whether you're a great boxer, Jack. George Gardner says you've got one hell of a punch, and Pete Eaton says you can take more punishment than any other fighter. And do you know what I say, Jack?'

Jack smiled lazily over his plate of ice-cream.

'I say the best thing you can do is punch yourself on the jaw for twenty rounds and then we'll see which one of them is right.'

Sadie had thought him good company. He had taken her down to the track next day and given her a couple sure-for-certain winners, one of which had won. 'And mind you, the other one was the good one.'

As far as Jack had known, that was all they had seen of each other. And now she had left him high and dry for Barty, as she had left the shipyard guy high and dry for himself, a little while back.

He sat down and put his head in his hands and cried. She was a bitch, and he never wanted to see her again, in his life. If he saw her, he would thrash the tripes out of her. She was a saint and his heart's darling and if he could ever find her again he would cherish her like a child.

Then he suddenly found himself thinking again of Barty. All he'd ever done for Barty was to roar with laughter at his damn-fool jokes and fill his glass with highballs. And all he'd ever done to-night to Sandy Ferguson, who was his friend, whom he loved, as far as you could love a white rival, was smash at his eyes with fists as hard as cannon-balls and hit him over the heart so hard he hoped his ribs might crack wide open.

He covered his wet eyes with his hands. Sandy Ferguson had landed punches that would have crushed rocks against his face and on his stomach: and all he had done was grin back at him. Yet now Sadie, so soft, so tender, had left him blubbering like a kid in pain.

Suddenly he sat up, the gusts of his grief having blown through him like a tornado. He remembered how Hank Griffin had driven him at will before him in the first few rounds of their first fight at Los Angeles, so that he had felt like a helpless kid buffeted at will by destiny. And yet he had stuck on. He had survived the buffeting; and he had ceased to be helpless. In the end, he had somehow broken even with Hank Griffin.

He got up. The first terrible round was over. He had been driven before the storm. From now on he was back in the middle of the ring storming his way to victory. Sadie couldn't escape him any more than Hank Griffin could. In life or in death she was his; he would find her and claim her.

As it turned out, it wasn't to be so easy. Porgy never set himself a harder problem. Old Tom from The Barbecue called next day with the first clue. They were over at Carmel in a little house near the Spanish church, and it was said the man beat her. He went over that night, determined on double murder: but nothing came of his visit. He found the house and the man and woman. He heard the screams and burst in the door. But they weren't Barty and Sadie: just two other crazy people, taking a pull at the great draught of sex and enjoying it, despite the screams. He tried Los Angeles and Colma and every race track about the State. The boys told him that when Barty described himself as a trainer—well, it was yes and no. Sometimes he trained regular and sometimes his owners changed their minds in the middle of the season, maybe in the middle of a meeting.

One day, his nephew Gus Rhodes came to talk to him about it.

'I've found her, Jack.'

'Like hell you've found her. All the guys I give a bottle of Scotch have found her. One in New Jersey, and one in Florida and one in Kentucky.'

'It's not like that, Jack. I've found her good and proper. Barty dumped her.'

'I don't believe it. There isn't a man in the wide world would dump Sadie.'

'Sure he did. He took her to Utah, then to Arizona. I found them at Tucson.'

He began to tell about his trip. Someone had said they were in a hunting lodge in the San Francisco yellow pine forests. They'd been there sure enough, honeymooning in a cabin—and then moved on to stay with one of Barty's owners on a great estate where alfalfa grew and date palms and figs. Gus had seen them on the veranda of a low white Colonial house near Yuma. 'But next day they'd gone. There was a race-meeting to Tucson, and Barty had a horse that couldn't lose.'

'So he dumped her,' said Jack skipping a few chapters.

'That old horse carried too much weight,' said Gus in excuse. 'It carried her ermine coat, and the ring and the necklace. It got beat a nose.'

'Where's he gone now?'

Gus spread his flat brown palms. 'Somebody said Nevada, somebody said across to Colorado. There was a man who said Barty had a wife at Phoenix. He always went back to her when they came unstuck.'

Jack shrugged. 'Who cares where he's gone? What's happened to Sadie?'

'She's in a cabaret show at Tucson. She sings and dances and if the customers buy drinks she keeps the cork and gets ten per cent on the bottle.'

Jack towered above him. 'Why in Christ's name didn't you bring her back?'

Gus hung his head. 'She wouldn't come.'

'Why didn't you make her?'

Gus sighed. He sat down on the bed Sadie had so often stretched out on. 'Give us a cigarette, Jack.' When he had blown out a mouthful of smoke he admitted sadly: 'Well, it was like this. I'd only single fare home. You see, I blued the rest on Barty's dead-sure-for-cert winner.'

That night Jack set off for Arizona. There was a fight he was pretty well fixed up for, but he turned that down. He couldn't wait till he'd seen Sadie again.

He went to the cabaret where she was dancing, and watched from the back of the hall. He'd have bet his bottom dollar she never spotted him.

When she came out into the deserted street a man was waiting for her. It was Barty. He slipped his arm into hers and led her to the carriage drawn up across the street. Jack followed them in the next on the line. In ten minutes' time he faced them across their hotel bedroom.

'So you didn't dump her after all?'

Bary was nonchalant and amused. 'Well, I did and I didn't. When that horse didn't do his duty by me, I stole her earrings and sold them for train-fare to Phoenix. I had to spend two nights there before my wife would lend me enough to get back with a bit over for a stake. And to-day I put the lot on and landed the jack-pot.' He dug his hands deep in his pocket and strewed dollar bills all over the bed.

'Help yourself, Mr Johnson, however much that fur coat cost you.'

Jack dropped his clenched fist to his side. This joker wasn't fit to be hit.

'Get your hat, Sadie. Unless he's stolen that from you too.'

'No market,' said Barty apologetically. 'You can't put a hat on a horse. God dammit, that's a song name.' He picked up a banjo beside the bed and began to strum.

Jack gripped Sadie by the arm. 'You're coming now.'

'But my things, Jack,' she whimpered, 'I must pack my things.'

'I'll get you more things.'

They shut the door of the hotel room on Barty sitting on the bed thrumming the banjo and trying to think up his new song. 'Hey, Jack,' he yelled after them. 'Go your bundle on Bee Sting at Phoenix, Thursday. Couldn't lose in a month of Sundays.'

They went out into the street. 'That's the end of him,' said Jack.

'If you ever see him again in your life, I'll throttle you.' The moon shone on a deserted street.

'Where are we going, Jack?'

'Home. Back to 'Frisco. Anywhere away from him.' He pulled her along roughly behind him.

'What's the good, Jack? He'll always be about. If it's not 'Frisco, it's L.A. He plays the horses all down the Coast. He's at everybody's party.'

He thought of Barty, sitting alone in that hotel bedroom. Next time they met, if there was a next time—he'd give him the old club handshake and start right away on '*You can't put a hat on a horse.*'

'He's all I'm worth,' she said. 'You'd never keep me. If it isn't Barty, it'd be someone else. I'd be for ever slipping out to some fancy man.'

He said savagely: 'We're going back to Chi. I'm through with the Coast. They all know me now—they can't duck me any more.

'And you—I'll find us an apartment fit for a duchess, and I'll have you watched there. If you ever speak to a man I'll sure beat the skin off you.'

It wasn't so easy breaking away from the Coast. There were fights that everyone expected would be fixed for the next couple of months and men who had to be cleared out of the way on his march to the top. There were plenty of boys in the gyms ready to whisper he was running out on them.

Moreover, when he reached Chicago, there wasn't all that much of a welcome waiting. Frank Childs was ready for the routine engagement. They boxed six rounds and Jack got the decision. But it was Frank's day all the same. When the contest was over, he held his hands up to the audience. 'Jack Johnson beat me to-day,' he bellowed, 'but he didn't knock me out. Nobody never done knock me out.' Then he blew a proud raspberry to the assembled company and vanished into the dressing-room.

Jack came home from the fight that night as lighthearted as he'd been for weeks. He'd make Sadie laugh for once in a while at least. Ever since they came to Chicago she'd sneered at him as soon as they got out of bed (up till then things went all right).

'You'll never keep me, Jack. You're a fool to try. You're your own worst enemy.'

'Why shouldn't I keep you? You've never been happier in your life than you are when you're in bed with me.'

'How do you know how happy I can be when you're not there?'

He snarled. 'If I thought that, I'd break someone's neck.'

'What good would that do you?'

She had been sitting in front of her mirror carefully making her face into a work of art. As she spoke, she coolly rubbed her hand across forehead, cheek and mouth leaving a smudged canvas in place of a masterpiece.

'Oh, who the hell cares about you? You want things all your own way. Knock out every man in the ring and knock out every woman in bed. That's the way you like it. And it never strikes you that's the way to get yourself hated by a woman.'

It didn't make sense, of course. She'd been crazy about him last night and he'd given her a fur muff and tippet that morning that were at least twice as expensive as the next best anyone in the gym had given his girl that season. A girl should reckon herself lucky with a guy that treated her that way.

He reached home full of the joy of life. She'd laugh when he told her Frank Childs' little gag. She couldn't help but laugh at that. The crowd had laughed its damn-fool face off, hadn't it?

This time he didn't suspect she had gone until he'd made himself at home and settled down with a glass of beer. Then he'd looked around and shouted and got no answer. When he'd finished his beer he got up and went into the bedroom. He lay down on the bed and shouted again. No answer. . . .

Then he knew. He knew as certainly as if she'd told him to his face. He got up and pulled open her drawers and cupboards. Empty of course—they would be. He smiled wryly at her cleverness in waiting till she got the fur muff and tippet. She'd timed her fade-out well.

Back in the sitting-room he found the drawer of his desk had been opened—he generally left the key in and never bothered. His savings were gone again, of course, every cent. He remembered the time he'd said he thought they might put their money into a bank; there was a boy down at the gym that did that and never seemed to be broke. How she'd laughed! So he was going to get careful, was he, in his old age? You had to go to him to ask for money for a new saucepan or a sausage. Jack Johnson, the cheese-parer; Jack Johnson the cheapskate! So they hadn't put the money in the bank. They'd left it there in the desk where anybody could get at it; and somebody had.

He didn't know where she'd gone this time, nor with whom. All he knew was that his life was empty, because she wasn't there. Somehow or other his instincts always told him to expect her the very minute after he'd remembered she had gone. He never went into another room without expecting to see her there. He hurt himself afresh over and over again with the witless hope that wouldn't die within him.

When he went down to train, his trainer met him with news of the great match he'd fixed up. 'Half a dozen more like this one and you'll be in line for the championship.'

'Skip it. I'm not in the mood for fights.'

'*Skip it?* What the hell! This is the break we've been waiting for. If you take this guy——'

'Not for me, thanks. Come to think of it, I don't feel like training this morning. Anyone like to come in on a pinochle game over a few bottles of cold beer?' And he went out into Chicago where there were half a million women, and the next one might be Sadie, but never was.

Next day he didn't bother to go to the gym at all; and the back pages began to hint that there wasn't going to be the big fight everyone had taken for granted and to wonder under their breaths whether Johnson was yellow.

He didn't care. He didn't care what they said about him. He took to loafing around town, especially down the streets he knew had been her favourites. Once he saw a girl who might have been Sadie go into a dress shop. He went in too. There was a department where they sold dresses and a department where they sold underclothes, but the girl wasn't in either of these. He finally found her in the department where they sold gloves. He stood in the doorway trying to get a good look at the face in the glass behind the counter, but he couldn't see her. Finally the saleswoman said something and the girl turned round. It wasn't Sadie.

A couple of weeks after, the man that ran the show at The Star came round one evening to suggest a little fight that wouldn't hurt a schoolboy. There was nice money in it, and the promise of a build-up; but he couldn't be bothered.

A little while after that, he did worse. He let them fix him up with a fight and then slid out of it a few days before he was due in the ring. Injured ribs, they said; but some of the papers remembered how the great little Negroes of a few years back hadn't minded going into a fight with a couple of broken ribs anyway.

It was a day or two after they'd called that fight off that he heard a man in the street say: 'That's Jack Johnson, the boxer. He's *finished*.'

Perhaps those were the words that saved him. He set his teeth and looked into the future. Suppose Sadie came back to-morrow, what would he have to show her? Neither victory, nor defeat . . . nothing but a long dull plain of inactivity. He must get to grips with the future.

He fought his way from East to West. It wasn't easy: no one any longer believed in him. In ten months he had one fight; and fortunately in that he knocked out his old rival Denver Ed Martin, who had proved such a big obstacle to Sam McVey on his abortive struggle towards the pinnacles. There was just enough money to be made out of knocking Martin for a loop to keep him in business on the Coast.

He was no longer a serious contender for championship honours. He hung about the gyms in search of pinochle games and about the race tracks in search of winners. Both the pinochle games and the bets on horses paid dividends. He couldn't find Sadie, but he could pick winners. He earned himself enough money to buy a ticket to New York. It was always possible that you would find Sadie in Harlem. You could search for her up and down the Coast and up and down the world and hear nothing of her, and then walk into a party in 152nd Street and there would be Sadie drinking gin and ether.

He was broke when he reached New York. He hadn't a couple of dimes to rub together; but he hadn't lost a match since Joe Choynski hit him on the temple four years earlier in Galveston. No one slouched around Times Square muttering out of the corner of his mouth that Jack Johnson was finished.

He hired the best flat in Harlem and nobody asked a sleek black panther for money in advance.

Nowadays, too, getting fights wasn't difficult. No one seemed to want him in New York City—perhaps the colour bar was too rigid—but out of town he became an immediate favourite. During 1905 he knocked out Walter Johnson, and Morris Harris in Philadelphia. He also beat Black Bill and Sandy Ferguson, losing during the year to Joe Jeannette on a foul. By Christmas time Jeannette was his major rival, but most of the experts didn't think that in the long run Joe was the likely candidate for world honours. The fights were fine: it was a good thing to stand toe-to-toe with the strongest men in the world swapping punches until someone withered in his tracks.

But where was Sadie, the girl upon whom his heart was set? He sought her everywhere, as he had sought her in Chicago. Always he looked for her in a green hat: the last time he had seen her wagging her hips down Michigan Avenue, she had been wearing one which in later years would have brought a smile of approval to the lips of Mr Michael Arlen. There wasn't a sign of Sadie. There were twenty-five green hats in Harlem one Saturday morning: on octoroons, quadroons, Negroes, white girls on a visit—all the girls in town. But none of them was on Sadie. You couldn't find Sadie uptown or downtown, in New Jersey or Long Island, in Brooklyn or in any of the Connecticut suburbs. Gus Rhodes couldn't find her or Charlie Chasehouse, the Chinese 'eye', or Bill Bruton, who was said to be as good as a hound on the trail, or old Ballo, the Australian black-tracker.

Did it matter? He wasn't dead any more: he faced the morning with confidence. There weren't any fights he would refuse—let them all come. But in the evenings, when training was over, he searched the town, his eyes held high on the hats of the women. Green hats everywhere—but none of them Sadie's.

The years passed. He grew up: he grew great. He reversed the decision against Jeannette; went to Australia to knock out Felix and Lang; came back to beat the ageing but hard-hitting Fitzsimmons. Burns became champion and, as we shall see, ambition blazed up in Jack to beat Burns and win the right to call himself the best man in the world. He chased Burns to England and on to Australia. In Sydney, on Boxing Day, 1908, he crowned the hopes of a lifetime by winning the world's title. Around his hotel next day ten score of girls gathered, to squeak with excitement when he went out, to blow him kisses and faint at the sight of him. Beautiful girls, voluptuous girls, desirable girls—but not Sadie.

He could beat any man in the world, but he couldn't find the one woman he wanted. Not in New York, or London, or Plymouth, or Paris, or Sydney. Nowhere.

The years passed. They dug Jim Jeffries out of his alfalfa farm and stacked him up against Jack at Reno. They searched for White Hopes who might do what Jeffries had not been able to do. Among the best of them was Ketchel and when Jack (as we shall see) had knocked the pulp out of Ketchel, he took time off to get married. He had forgotten the girl in the green hat. If he saw Sadie in the street, he wasn't sure that he would recognize her; but when he met her in dreams they knew each other as if they had never been parted.

He wasn't paying any attention when a horse-player from Chicago said to him at a party, 'Jack, you and Sadie were friends once. What are you going to do about her now?'

'Sadie?' The name didn't register. Who in hell was Sadie?

'Don't you ever read the papers, Jack?'

'Sure I do. Joe Jeannette boxed a No Decish with Big Sam over at——'

'Don't you ever read anything except the back page?'

'Who does?'

'You're dead right,' said another crap-player to the racing man. 'A guy who reads only the back page never reads the world's news at all. Such a man is strictly a bum. An intellectual, a true citizen of the world we live in, he steeps himself in what is front page news. 'Cos why? 'Cos what is front page news to-day is history to-morrow.'

The horse-player pulled a paper out of his pocket. 'That's right,' he said. He read: '*Sex-starved Moron slays Four. Pawns Hatchet to Buy Dance Ticket.*' 'How's that?' He turned the paper back. '*Sugar Daddy Faces Gross Indecency Rap.*'

'*Woman Boils, Eats Baby.*'

'*Love Nest Queen Slays Heart-Throb.*'

'*Senator says American Girl heads World League in Grace, Beauty.*'

'Here it is,' he said. '*Coloured Girl Booked for Murder.*'

'*Did She Slay Brother?*'

Jack said slowly: 'That wasn't Sadie?'

'Who knows?' said the horse-player. 'They've locked her up for it anyway. Maybe they're wrong?'

'They're wrong. Where did all this happen?'

'Over at New Jersey.'

Next day he saw Sadie again for the first time in five years. She had changed. There was a scornful defiance about her greeting. 'Sit down, Jack. There is never any shortage of chairs in this gaol. Why, they told me when I came in that even if the worst happened I could be sure of a seat.'

He gazed at her as if she surpassed belief. He wasn't amazed that she might have killed her brother. He was trying to understand how she could ever have left him. *That* was a crime; cold-blooded and ruthless: the other—if it had ever happened—could only have been an accident, or a flash of fury. Anyone might murder anybody. But only a she-devil would have left a man as she had left him.

Well, there wasn't much he could do now. He couldn't take her back—there was his wife in her place. It was all over for Sadie. Of course he would see that she got a lawyer who would plead her cause. Oh yes, he would see that she got off. But what good would that be to her—to be restored, as it were, to life-in-death. Perhaps it would be better if he left her to die, rather than restore her to life without him.

'Christ, Jack, you look as if it was *you* they'd got locked up. What's biting you?'

He took her hand. 'Sadie, my darling, I've got to tell you this. You must be brave about it, as brave as I've ever had to be in a fight. The thing is this—I can get you a lawyer who'll spring you, sure enough. But what good are life and liberty going to be to you? You see, Sadie darling, I'm no longer free to look after you, to have you back. You got to know—*I'm a married man*.'

She snatched her hand from his and crammed it into her mouth. She swayed, she leaned against the prison wall; then she fell back on her bed and rolled from one side to the other, helpless with laughter.

'It was hysterics, of course,' Jack explained to his wife when he told her the story.

'Of course.'

'Anyway I'll get the mouthpiece for her. When the case is over, we'll set her up in—oh, in a restaurant or something. She always said she'd like to run a restaurant.'

And a restaurant it was, after she left the court without a stain on her character. Jack used to eat turkey and all the trimmings there every Thanksgiving Day. He was glad the place was prosperous, of course, but it somehow offended him that Sadie should be so remarkably expert at concealing the heart-break with which she must be stricken.

And there was another thing. She never wore a green hat nowadays. When he asked her why not, she said her head-waiter told her it didn't suit her complexion.

V

◆◆◆

THE FACT WAS that by 1906 he had beaten the best of them, and beaten them so convincingly that he had a right to tackle the one man he couldn't get into the ring for the championship. Anyway, who was this Tommy Burns, and what right had he to call himself champion of the world? That was the question Sam Fitzpatrick, Jack's manager, was never tired of asking everybody, especially journalists, who once in a long while could be persuaded to echo his curiosity in their columns.

The real trouble was that there hadn't been (at least in Fitzpatrick's opinion) a genuine proven champion since Jeffries. When Jeffries retired unbeaten in 1904, someone had to take over the title. In the ordinary way, the sensible thing would have been to stage a competition for the honour, but Jeffries so dominated the scene that he had been allowed to name his own terms as to the choice of his successor. His view was that a fight between Marvin Hart and Jack Root would settle the question as to who was the best man in the world—next to the referee, who happened to be himself. The winner had been Marvin Hart, and his was a name with which opponents of Fitzpatrick could temporarily silence Johnson's manager, while he tried hard to think of an answer. For the fact was that, though most people professed to regard Hart as an unproven champion, the new boss had given one proof at least—he had shown himself a better man than Johnson.

The two had fought in San Francisco in 1904, when Jack, though twenty-six years of age, had not quite reached the peak of his form. It had been a dour struggle for twenty rounds and Alex Greggains' decision in favour of the white man from Kentucky had certainly not been welcomed by most of the spectators. For the first eight rounds Johnson, it was true, had boxed with foxy cunning, but generally without aggression. There had been only one moment when he had come to life; and that had been in the sixth round when a couple of straight lefts had knocked Hart clear across the ring and almost through the ropes. But though he had had the better of the in-fighting that had then developed, and though he had marked his

53

man with bloodied eyebrows and crimson gashed lips, he could never put him down.

More than once before the fifteenth round was over, Johnson gazed beseechingly at the referee, hoping he could be induced to stop the fight. It would have saved a lot of trouble. As it was, all because of that official's heartlessness, Johnson found himself subjected to the most frightful battery of body blows all through the sixteenth and seventeenth rounds. John Arthur Johnson was swept from neutral corner to neutral corner: moreover Hart's offensive did not blow itself out at the end of these two rounds. He continued to attack remorselessly till the end of the fight. Through half-closed eyes he pin-pointed his target: somehow he raised exhausted arms and conjured them into pistons to pump forth destruction. The last three rounds of the fight all belonged to Marvin Hart: nevertheless it was a surprise when the referee decided that the fight belonged to him too.

As for Jack Johnson, he was more than surprised; he was shocked. His view was that this was one further move made by the Jeffries' camp to hold him at bay. Hart was known to the world at large as Jeffries' protégé. Johnson's feeling was that a decision for Hart was a vote for Jeffries: a re-assurance to the world that the title-holder didn't have to revise his decision that there was no valid reason for him to have to tackle the Galveston Negro.

And a couple of years after Marvin Hart's possibly fortunate decision over him, the Kentucky boxer earned his arbitrarily decided claim to the title by knocking out Jack Root in the twelfth round. There were plenty of men who followed the fight game who declared that Hart had no more claim to the crown than had Peter Maher after Corbett had attempted to hand it to him on a plate when he himself proposed to retire in '96. Most of them would not have pointed to Johnson as the logical contender, in spite of the eloquence of Sam Fitzpatrick. There were better claimants than he, in spite of the fact that since being beaten by Hart the Galveston man had abandoned the Pacific Coast for the East where he had won a series of victories that put him in line for consideration as a claimant to the title. The experts wanted to know why Jeffries had ignored the claims, in particular, of Philadelphia Jack O'Brien and of Tommy Burns, born Noah Brusso, late of Canada.

Of the two, perhaps O'Brien commanded more respect. He was a light-heavyweight who held the title in his own class, having knocked out Bob Fitzsimmons in thirteen rounds, but he was totally uninterested in hitting men of his own size. In time to come he was to fight a no-decision bout with Johnson, though it must be mentioned that in two contests with the middleweight Ketchel he once barely escaped being knocked out and once did not escape at all.

Perhaps O'Brien's best performance in the ring was in that no-decision six-rounder in Philadelphia against Johnson, between the latter's victory over Burns and before his match with Jeffries. O'Brien was easily the master in this contest; but it must be mentioned that Johnson took advantage of the fact that no verdict could be given under the local rules to take the ring grossly overweight and palpably untrained.

But before Johnson reached his peak, O'Brien had his day. He had certain very good grounds for considering himself hardly treated by Jeffries' arbitrary decision to hand over the heavyweight title to the winner of the Hart-Root contest. Six months before this match he himself had knocked out Bob Fitzsimmons, Jeffries' predecessor, in thirteen rounds at San Francisco. If it came to that he had beaten Burns on points in Milwaukee, though Burns had a series of excuses for this defeat which even among boxers must rank as remarkable. Chief among them was his belief that he was due to fight a middleweight, like himself, by the name of Hugo Kelly. Imagine his astonishment when he arrived in town (after four days on the train from Seattle) to find that his opponent was not to be Kelly but the redoubtable Jack O'Brien himself! At that time O'Brien had not tasted defeat in the hundred and thirty fights he had crowded into the past four years, and he had knocked out Jack Twin Sullivan in three rounds and battled in no-decision bouts with Choynski, Kid McCoy, Tommy Ryan, Hart and Walcott.

Burns, however (and he always felt that this was one of the particularly fine deeds his unselfish nature provoked him to commit), agreed to fight O'Brien at three days' notice, possibly being persuaded to this course by O'Brien's personal assurance that at the end of six rounds the referee had got his instructions to declare the fight a draw. And then—after all his selfless readiness to fall in with other people's plans—the hapless Burns was double-crossed. The referee gave an honest decision after all: and gave it to O'Brien. No wonder that Burns was incensed years later when Philadelphia Jack was strutting round and claiming that he had a better right to the title than Marvin Hart.

The American press was behind O'Brien, but strangely enough

neither the papers nor the boxer clamoured for a match with Burns
even after the latter had beaten Hart, to clear up the question of
precedence beyond argument. Both press and boxers were content
to give their solemn assurance that Philadelphia Jack O'Brien was
the best man in the world, and leave it at that. But in due course a
promoter came into the picture and paid O'Brien enough money to
lure him into the ring with Burns at Los Angeles. Here Burns did
everything that was required, except get the verdict.

One of O'Brien's friends had the temerity to say to him next
morning: 'What are you beefing about, Timmy? You're always
grumbling that the referee doesn't give you a draw. And now when
he does, you aren't satisfied.'

Nor were the press and the public. Both were of the opinion that
Burns had won everything but the decision. All they asked was one
more fight to settle the matter for good.

For some time the project hung fire. O'Brien was less than eager
to submit his claims to yet another referee, but when Burns stalked
him down in a Los Angeles cigar store and taunted him with
cowardice it was no longer possible to resist the challenge. The two
men were matched for the third time, with the acknowledged
world's championship as the most important part of the prize.

As Burns told it, the signing of the contract was only one of the
difficulties he had to face before undertaking the comparatively
simple task of beating O'Brien in the ring. Soon enough came an
invitation to join Philadelphia Jack and a few of his friends over a
cup of coffee. After they had discussed the weather, these gentlemen had a curious proposition to put to the champion of the world.
Their suggestion was that he should lie down in the eleventh or the
thirteenth round (whichever looked the more convincing as the fight
worked out), and that he should sign a paper guaranteeing a thousand
dollars as proof that he would keep his word to throw the fight.
Burns signed; no doubt his reason for doing so was that he was desperately in need of the money he would get from forcing O'Brien
into the ring and he saw no other way of bringing about this desirable
consummation.

But then a complication arose. When the stipulated date arrived,
on which Burns must find the money to deposit as an honourable
guarantee of his intended dishonesty, he found himself unable to
raise anything. No wonder the champion felt indignant! Things
had come to a pretty pass when the best man on earth couldn't raise
a paltry thousand bucks to endorse his word of honour (which no one

had ever dared question) that he was proposing to throw a fight. There was a serious fear that the contest might be called off. Fortunately, however, Burns was not quite without friends. A steadfast ally was found who put up the money and handed it over in notes to O'Brien's backers. True (as Burns told it), the notes were forgeries; but the O'Brien party never rumbled this. Burns had kept his word; and the fight was on again.

What is more, it was of course *really* on. Burns had no intention whatever of lying down in the eleventh, thirteenth, or any other round. He had said he would, he had signed a document pledging himself to do so, simply to make sure of getting O'Brien into the ring, a necessary preliminary to drawing his own share of that much-needed purse. Meanwhile, in the last few weeks before the contest the bets had come pouring in on O'Brien. The fly boys knew all about the little arrangement and had backed Philadelphia Jack so heavily that he started the fight at 2-1 on.

When the men went into the ring, Burns at once went up to the referee and told him that he intended to keep straight with the public and consequently would be grateful if he would announce that all bets made on O'Brien to win *up till that time* were to be declared null and void. The referee stared. Such an announcement could only mean one thing: that there had been a cross; that this cross was double-crossed, and that from then on backers were given their chance to pick the winner in a straight fight.

The referee held up his hands for silence. He cupped his palms. His voice carried as though through a megaphone against a background of stunned silence. 'Gentlemen, all bets made on O'Brien to win up to this moment are off. The fight will now commence. Gentlemen, you are free to make your bets now as you will.'

The bell rang for the first round. O'Brien stood in his corner as if thunderstruck, his back to the ring. Burns dashed across to him, spun him round and as they clinched whispered in his ear: 'Fight your best, Jack. I'm out to beat you now I've got you here at last. This is a real fight.'

Not many seconds had passed before O'Brien knew all too well that this was true. In their last contest Burns had *boxed* so that he showed all his considerable scientific skill and especially the elegant footwork of which he was a past-master. He did not box now—he fought. He fought like a wild-cat. He threw his punches from all angles. A right hook crashed behind O'Brien's ear; three straight lefts landed with rattling speed over the heart—as Jack backed away

he took a rolling swing to the jaw, as he ducked, an uppercut shook
him to his foundations.

Burns hated O'Brien, but he did not underrate him. He considered that in boxing finesse, speed and sheer cleverness, Philadelphia Jack O'Brien was as good as any man in the world. Years
later, in retirement, he went on record as rating him as better than
Jack Johnson as a swift mover and as a stylist. But when it came to
hurtful punching and non-stop aggression he was confident that
O'Brien must admit that he was his master.

And so it was to prove. Burns's crude fury carried the day from
the first bell. O'Brien was bewildered. All his artistry knew no
defence against this rough-housing. If he blocked a left hand, it was
ten to one his jaw was jolted out of joint by the right elbow that
followed it; if he sought escape in a clinch he found himself mauled
as if by a grizzly bear. Burns nearly knocked him out in the fifth
round, kidding him to counter-attack and then nailing him with a
right hand punch like a blast of dynamite. It was a high tribute to
O'Brien's beautiful gameness that he weathered the frightful assault
on his feet. Even so, when the final bell sounded, there could be no
doubt in the world that Tommy Burns was the winner and the best
heavyweight on the earth.

Only Jack Johnson remained unconvinced. He began to talk
louder and louder, and the substance of what he said remained un-
altered. He desired to let the world know that he was better than
Burns. He expressed, through his manager, an eloquent if dis-
approving opinion of the little Napoleon, who stood a bare five feet
seven inches and weighed a mere hundred and eighty pounds.

Burns chose to take no notice of his taunts, beyond drawing the
colour line a little bit tighter. He contented himself with pointing
out that he was a fighting champion. He didn't wait for challengers
with big money to bet on themselves. He travelled the world to
meet the world's best. After he had completely established his right
to the title (technically his without a doubt after his victory over
Marvin Hart), he knocked out Bill Squires of Australia in a single
round and then set sail for England. There wasn't, to be truthful, a
great deal of opposition to be encountered in England's green and
pleasant land. The best of a poor bunch was Gunner Moir, a
modest, quiet person who touched his forelock when the world's
champion condescended to speak to him. It was only Moir's docile
behaviour that made a match at the National Sporting Club a
possibility. Burns was calm and suave, but hard as iron when it

came to a business deal. He had certain clear-cut views about the sort of boxing gloves he proposed to wear. He had his own ideas of who was to referee.

Worst of all, he had very strong views about how the purse was to be handled—before he accepted delivery of it. The two men were fighting for £2,500, and Burns (he was later suitably apologetic) had the impudence to refuse to go into the ring before he had seen the colour of the National Sporting Club's money. Nothing so audacious had ever been heard in that sacred building since the days when, as Evans's, it served as a model for Thackeray's great scene in *The Newcomes*. It is certain that 'Peggy' Bettinson would have ordered the fellow off the premises but for the fact that the Gunner had some rights to a bashing after his kindly and accommodating behaviour. So in the end the money was produced in notes, and Burns had a good look at it. As for the side stakes of £500, they were handed over to Eugene Corri, the referee, to put into his dinner-jacket pocket until after the fight. Corri got hot pulling the men apart in the third or fourth round and took off his coat and flung it over the ropes for somebody to look after until the bout was over. Then—as anybody but Burns would have known—the money was found intact, and handed over to the winner.

And the winner of course was Burns. He was two and a half inches the shorter and a stone the lighter man; but his reach was the greater and from the first bell he used it to make a fool of his magnificent, heavily tattooed opponent. He led and missed, slipped the counter-punch and lured Moir to grab his head till Corri broke the men apart and warned the Englishman that if there was any more of this rough stuff he would be disqualified.

Outside in Covent Garden a great crowd waited and the buzz went round the crowd that things were going badly already. But inside, the men at the ringside were looking puzzled. Was *this* the celebrated world-beater? He didn't look it! He looked like nothing very important at all; he looked like a spoiler without a punch. There were several moments when Moir appeared wide open and this square little chap with the hair *à la Bonaparte* and the glittering blue eyes never seemed aware that he had him at his mercy. And this in spite of the fact that from time to time Burns would cast a pitying eye at the husky Gunner. It was generally known that he had £500 to back himself with to win this fight; but the way he was going about it suggested that he was ready to push the odds up while there was still time.

But as the rounds went by the golden merits of Burns became dazzlingly apparent. In the third round he took the fight to close quarters and shook the thick-built Gunner with a whole salvo of half-arm jabs before which he reeled and finally sank in a heap. True, he was up again soon enough, but he was puffing like a grampus and only succeeded in hugging his way to the haven of the interval between rounds.

Thereafter, it was all Burns. The Napoleonic eye gleamed, the black locks were shaken into place after each ruffling interchange of compliments in a neutral corner. Above all, the long arms flashed and gashed. The Gunner's heaving breath came in even shorter spasms. In the stalls the patrician jaws sunk lower on the gleaming shirt fronts: the hoarse whispers in gas-lit Covent Garden outside the Club front door sank even lower in despondency. For round after round the champion toyed with a challenger not so much as a cat toys with a mouse but rather as the Ironies play with the protagonist of a tragedy. He skipped clear of the Gunner's floundering rushes, ducked the ponderous swings, slipped the leaden leads. And he planted his own stinging blows at will, until in the tenth round he came to the conclusion that he had entertained the distinguished company long enough and wreaked summary execution upon poor Moir.

Hard luck, Gunner! Before he fought Burns he had beaten some fair performers: Jack Casey and Ben Taylor, Jack Palmer and Tiger Smith. After his defeat, he was to be beaten in eight of the nine fights that lay ahead of him before he retired from the ring to appear in British films, generally in a small part as an executioner. This, with the Gunner's black-avised, lowering countenance was straightforward type-casting. But on the night of 25 February 1907, at the National Sporting Club, Gunner James Moir did not look like an executioner—quite the contrary.

After his defeat of Moir, Burns was left with a poor opinion of English boxers if with a high regard for the honesty of the aristocracy. A sparring-match with J. W. H. T. Douglas, later England cricket captain and one-time Olympic middleweight champion, made him pause for reflection on the former point. Douglas had a classic style, the courage of a Spartan, and enough character to refuse to be withered by one glance of a blue, Napoleonic eye. Burns was breathing as hard as the Gunner himself at the end of three hectoring rounds, and at first was inclined to be fruitily indignant about the buffeting that had been wished on him when he was virtually unprepared. Suddenly, however, with a magnanimity that would have done credit to a Press lord, he decided that the Napoleonic thing to do was to be eloquently generous. 'If this is what you call a sparring exhibition,' he jovially proclaimed, 'what is your honest-to-God fighting like down here?'

Burns took part in several fights against minimus opponents before he left what in those days used to be the British Isles. In Wonderland he kept the dazzled East Enders from their jellied eels while he allowed Jack Palmer to clutch him as a child clutches his nurse—until putting him gently to sleep in the fourth round. The fantastic thing about that particular performance was that it ever took place. To-day you will sometimes hear of a great actor who takes a refresher course at the Old Vic, but never of a world's champion who amuses himself by taking on the local talent in a boxing programme at a suburban Baths.

After he had allowed Palmer to last four rounds, Burns, like a kind-hearted schoolmaster who knows that discipline must be maintained, made an example of Jem Roche on St. Patrick's Day in Dublin in eighty-eight seconds.

If Roche failed to make a name to stagger humanity out of this fight, at least one Irishman turned it to good account. As the roar went up that signalled Roche's instantaneous defeat, he ran as if for his life for the exit, flourishing his ticket above his head. 'I can't bear to look at it,' he howled, 'Roche is after murdering him. Is there anyone here who could bear to witness the horrid spectacle? He can buy my ticket for two pounds—cash.'

Burns was staying at the Dolphin Hotel and as he left to go to the Theatre Royal for the fight he made a bet of £700 that he would win and be back for supper in half an hour. He won with minutes to spare.

Burns left for Australia shortly afterwards, stopping off in Paris on the way. He made a monkey out of Jewey Smith, and then knocked out 'Bosker' Bill Squires, a rugged Australian whose spiritual home was the eighteenth century, and who on this occasion lasted eight rounds with the champion.

In Australia, Burns came under the control of Hugh D. McIntosh. 'Huge Deal' was a remarkable man. In his time he was a racing cyclist, a boxer who trained under Larry Foley (who founded the game in Australia under the auspices of Jem Mace), a waiter, a newspaper proprietor, an M.P., the chief theatrical impresario in his country, the founder of the milk-bar industry in England, the owner of Kitchener's house in Hampstead (whither he imported Bulli wickets for week-end games), and the first promoter of fights in the era of Big Purses. He was the first man to flirt with the merits of Bombardier Wells; and the first man to bring women and evening dress to the ringside when he matched the Bombardier against a string of less than first-class opponents in the Olympia Annexe.

One of his great feats in Australia was to buy up all the flags in the Commonwealth and New Zealand just before the American fleet arrived; so that his Government, anxious to give an official welcome, had to buy every square foot of bunting from him, at his own price.

He also built the Rushcutters Bay Stadium, which ranks to-day with Madison Square Garden, Harringay and the Vel d'Hiver as a historic home of the fight game. He could not find a banker to subsidize his venture, so he borrowed the slats of wood of which the Stadium was built, from a timber yard, promising to give them back as soon as his season of boxing contests was over. As it happened, he made his fortune; the Stadium has stood as a memorial to his foresight and initiative ever since.

VI

◆◆

BURNS ARRIVED IN SYDNEY to fight Squires and Lang. He beat them both, though Squires gave him plenty of difficulty, chiefly because the champion happened to be suffering from a severe attack of influenza when he went into the ring for this contest. For several rounds he was quite unable to focus and hit out in the general direction of the whereabouts of the challenger, as reported by his own trustworthy ears. Sometimes he hit him; sometimes he missed by a mile. In the thirteenth round he hit him: indeed he hit him so hard that it was unnecessary to keep his ears open for Squires' whereabouts any longer.

Soon after Burns had left for Australia, Jack Johnson arrived in London. He was handled by Sam Fitzpatrick, and whatever may be said about his subsequent behaviour, Jack on this occasion was docile almost to the point of obsequiousness.

'Stay here, Jack,' said Fitzpatrick when the two of them reported at the National Sporting Club in Covent Garden, 'stay here until I send for you.'

'Right here on the mat, Mr Fitzpatrick,' promised Jack; and there he stayed to be whistled at by London errand boys until the white men sent for him to show his paces in a sparring bout. But once 'Peggy' Bettinson had seen Jack in action he had no doubt what would happen as soon as he brought the champion to book. He immediately attempted to get the match for London. He offered Burns £2,500 to defend his title against the Negro, but Burns laughed at the suggestion. It was probable that he knew full well that that if he undertook this fight it was the last chance he would have of battling for a big purse. At supper, on the evening after his defeat of Moir, he had said to Euguene Corri, the referee, 'They want me to fight that nigger, Jack Johnson. I shall want £6,000 win, or lose or draw, and I don't suppose any promoter will give that amount. But if they do, I will give him the fight of his life, *although I don't think I can beat him.*'

Now at last a promoter was found to take this fantastic chance. In faraway Australia, where no one had even supposed enough money existed to pay for outsize purses, Hugh D. McIntosh was ready to meet Burns's demands. He had already seen both fighters in action, for Johnson had followed Burns to Australia on the champion's first visit and won the respect of the fighting fraternity by his victories over the gigantic Peter Felix and the local hero, Bill Lang. Since then, there had been, in America, the triumph in a couple of rounds over Fitzsimmons, a shell of the historic figure of a decade earlier; and the visit to England when Johnson had knocked out Ben Taylor in Plymouth, after playing with him for eight rounds. It was no unknown claimant whom McIntosh at last invited to tackle Burns in a championship contest, but a man who was already acclaimed by the press of the world as the logical contender for the title.

As for the conditions of the fight, Burns demanded and got his £6,000, win, lose or draw. At first Jack was prepared to take any pittance McIntosh named as all the reward he needed—in fact, if he had had anything in the bank, he would probably have paid for the privilege of being allowed to force the champion to defend his title. With Fitzpatrick, he made the most elaborate calculations as to what the contest was likely to draw, but as Boxing Day, 1908, drew nearer it became clear that his reckoning was very far short of reality. From that time onward Johnson was morose and unpleasant to deal with. He had, it appeared, forgotten to include McIntosh's cut of the motion picture rights, and he couldn't forgive himself.

In the matter of the choice of referee he proved almost impossibly exacting. Name after name was put forward: Corri of England, the leading American referees, 'Snowy' Baker of Australia who was to give J. W. H. T. Douglas such a heroic battle in the final of the 1908 Olympic middleweights. Any one of them was good enough for Burns, none of them was acceptable to Johnson. At last, when the boxers were arguing heatedly, Jack turned to McIntosh and put the point in language an infant could digest: 'Listen, Mr Mac, it's like this. I know that for every point scored to me I'll have earned two: because I'm a Negro. I want to be sure I get one point anyway. There's only one man I know I can trust to give it to me—and that man is yourself.'

It was not an easy position for McIntosh, who, in the first place, did not pretend to be a specialist on the finer points of the game; and who, secondly, was at least a sufficiently good judge to have flown in the face of public opinion by heavily backing Johnson to win. How-ever, both men declared themselves satisfied with their referee, and McIntosh spent several hours after his day's work in the booking office making himself familiar with the Queensberry Rules.

Johnson was truculent and unbearable as soon as he knew that Burns was committed to the fight. On the morning of the contest he announced that he would not go into the ring until his share of the purse was handed over. McIntosh unlocked a drawer of his desk and produced, not the gate money, but a loaded revolver; and Jack rapidly changed his mind.

Both men were magnificently trained for the historic occasion. Burns was a light-heavyweight by modern standards: he usually weighed 12 st. 6 lb. at his fighting peak, but his great reach—seventy-four inches—attracted general admiration. Moreover everyone was impressed by his experience. For the fight of his life at Rush-cutters Bay, he had actually trained himself down to 12 st. $\frac{1}{2}$ lb.: for once no one could accuse him of being a trifle on the fat side. Johnson, too, was fine drawn: he tipped the beam at 13 st. 10 lb., over a stone less than he had weighed when he went into training.

The fight of the century was scheduled to take place at 11 a.m. on 26 December 1908. Hugh McIntosh's vast stadium to-day is crowned with a roof which is shaken by the roars of cheering as the big fights follow each other, week after week, in the long roll-call of history. There was no roof in 1908. McIntosh hadn't been able to borrow enough wood to run to a roof. But even if there wasn't a roof, that didn't mean you could scramble in during the night over the walls and hide under a seat until dawn came to dazzle the eyes that glanced across the road at the white sails upon the little yachts bobbing in the Bay. One or two tried and were carried out on stretchers. All night long the crowd had streamed down from the heights of Darlinghurst. The Greek steak-and-oyster merchants, the Italian fruit-sellers, the French chefs and waiters in the most cosmopolitan suburb in the world had become *afficionados* for the day. As for the Sydney-siders born and bred—well, for once nobody was interested in the two o'clock winner at Randwick, or what was happening in the day's pony racing, or at the trots.

Christmas Day was no family holiday in one household out of four. At about the time that Dad was expected to be taking his place at the head of the table to carve the turkey, he was reported missing with any son who had reached his teens. If you searched the little streets round the Stadium, you would find them all sitting around in the gutter, waiting for the gates to open next morning. There were kids with a pound between them who had borrowed the family yacht to sail five hundred miles along the coast to be in Sydney, if not in the Stadium, on the day of the fight. Many a sundowner had waltzed Matilda all the way from Melbourne or Brisbane.

And, of course, One-Eyed Connolly was there. No one knew how the most famous tramp alive had bummed his way into the country, but he had always said that if a ship's cat could travel the world he was capable of doing as much himself. And he had certainly earned (if *earned* is the word) his entrance money in a manner that was a model of ingenuity, if not of strict commercial honesty. He had gone to a fruit shop a couple of days before the fight and peering anxiously at the gooseberries offered him had lost his glass eye which must have fallen out of its socket on to the floor. A frantic search failed to find it, and at last Connolly went away, almost weeping out of his remaining orb. It was a thing, he said, he wouldn't have had happen for £10 as he'd have to pay at least that for a replacement from New York, the only place that could really make an eye to his measurements. Anyway, he'd call in that evening to see whether, by any chance, the eye had turned up.

And five minutes after he left the shop the eye *did* turn up. A gentleman came in to buy a pound of gooseberries and found it staring unwinkingly at him from among the fruit. At first he was inclined to regard it as his own property (otherwise the greengrocer must surely have given him short weight) but in the end he was persuaded to part with it for a fiver. The only curious part of the story, to the innocent fruiterer at least, was that Connolly never turned up that evening to claim his eye—which was in any event one of a job lot he had bought for half a dollar. But anyone scanning the bleacher on the morning of the great fight might have spotted Connolly and the later customer at the greengrocer's sitting side by side in the fifty shilling seats.

Yes, everyone was there who could raise the price of a seat and a ticket to Sydney. And in faraway Hanover, Ontario, they were staying up all night to get the first news in the morning papers of the victory of Canada's son. In the lamp-lit reporters' room of the Calcutta daily the young sports editor played hand after hand of poker while the punkah swung slowly below the lizard-thick ceiling and the tepid beer on the table grew hot as soup. In the little houses around the Louisiana cotton-fields Negroes prayed and wept and had visions. In Harlem they were dancing all night, and in New Orleans too, to a new music which had the throb of the jungle's heartbeat in its blood and its eyes bright flickers of hope and, now and then, the glaze of infinite despair.

The race was awake after so long a sleep of hopelessness. The race was on the march—for hope shone, paler and further away than dawn above the far horizon. The race was on the march! The shuffle of weary feet in the cotton-fields. The strut of young bucks in brilliantly gas-lit Harlem. The lope of leopard men in the jungle. Drums were beating in the blood. The spears of hope flashed in the pale light of dawn. A new world was over the horizon. A new word, a new life, a new dignity—for the Negro.

And yet, so far, the Negro hid his hopes as a secret hugged to his heart. Few of Johnson's race were at the ring-side to give him backing against the towering crowd of white men, behind Burns to a man and to a shilling. They had made him favourite at the fantastic odds of 7–4 on. Jack's smile grew thin and sour at the news. 'It's the best chance I'll ever have of cleaning up, Sam,' he said bitterly to Fitzpatrick. 'And I haven't a pound. We owe the hotel bill still.'

'We'll pay it to-night,' Fitzpatrick answered buoyantly. 'What's a hotel bill to a world's champion?'

Seven to four on—and hard to get your money invested! Pat O'Keefe, Burns's sparring partner was in his corner, the husky British middle-weight who was to give Billy Wells a hard scrap for his title and take the ring against Carpentier. He knew just how good the champion was and thought him a moral certainty. It was the in-fighting that Pat relied on. He'd never come across such deadly, hard-hitting, close-quarters stuff before in all his puff—and puff was the operative word.

There was another good reason to feel confidence in Burns; and that reason was Burns's confidence in himself. The police were to be at the ringside and it was known that they were by no means prepared to sit in at a massacre. If the fight became totally one-sided (or perhaps for some other unspecified reason) the police would certainly stop it. What was to happen then? Was the bout to be declared a No Contest, or was the referee empowered to give a points decision on the evidence before him? The alternatives were put before Burns, as champion, and he promptly voted for a referee's decision. *That* showed, as nothing else could, how he expected the fight to go.

And now the day had come. Burns, it was quickly reported, had slept like a log and had to be forcibly awakened at 8 a.m. (It was all right his being forcibly awakened, so long as he was not forcibly put to sleep.) His friends and camp followers had helped him to while away the time with community singing. Those who had heard them rendering 'Where the River Shannon Flows' vowed that his spirits could not have been higher.

And so, at long last, to the ringside. It was, indeed, a prodigious battle to get as far as this. There were 20,000 men inside the Stadium, while twice as many thronged the streets. Observe, that the *mot juste* for this crowd is *men*; and yet it is not altogether accurate, for there are two women among those 20,000 spectators. Only two pioneers! Why, when John L. Sullivan was rolling them over, one of his girl-friends used to come and watch him fight regularly; though it must be admitted that she attended disguised as a young man. Who were the two women who came to watch Burns and Johnson—and why did no journalist of the day apparently take the trouble to interview either of them afterwards?

Meanwhile, all eyes were on the boxers in their respective corners. There was a sharp general intake of breath as Johnson threw off his gorgeous dressing-gown. The Negro stripped like a superman, there was no doubt of that. His shoulders were splendidly muscled; his long arms had the look of heroic strength. He did not, as many champions do, taper away to nothing in the legs. He had enough legs to have run for his life: but his gleaming smile did not suggest that he had the least intention of doing any such thing.

The queer thing was Johnson could smile like a playboy when his heart was full of malice. There he was, smiling now at the referee, while he gestured towards Burns's corner. Surely there was nothing wrong now—now at this eleventh hour before a contest which had taken all the world's wits and wiles to bring about? Yet there was. Burns was wearing on his right forearm a bandage to protect a muscle wrenched in training. 'Make him take it off, Mr Mac,' drawled the Negro. 'Make him take it off at once—or I quit the ring.'

Hugh McIntosh had been through much to bring the men together. A dozen times he had had to threaten Johnson with a black jack around which a roll of music had been wrapped, before he could persuade him to accept some perfectly straightforward feature of the arrangements. Now, after having been forced to order him into the ring at pistol-point he was in no mood to listen to further badinage.

'Either you come out fighting when the bell goes, or the fight's off—and you are disqualified.'

'Mr Mac, either he takes off that bandage, or I don't come out of my corner.'

There was a minute to go before the bell. Johnson put his dressing gown over his shoulders again. Burns shrugged—then with a nonchalant gesture wrenched the bandage from his arm. The bell rang. The men came out fighting.

It is 11.15 on an Australian midsummer morning. The sun blazes down. The crowd sucks in its breath. Johnson springs across the ring, there is a flurry of punches, a clinch, a feint with the left, and Burns's jaw is unprotected for a split second. Of all the great punches Johnson carries in his armoury, the right uppercut is the greatest and most unanswerable. Every other boxer from Figg to the latterday champions has signalled the punch, has used his feet. Not so Johnson. It is his great gift to smash home the heaviest punch he carries without moving his feet, steady as a rock—even bending forward, his head out towards his opponent. Any other boxer who attempted this magic blow was certain to fall flat on his face; Johnson could always put all his weight into it, and retain the mobility of a featherweight if called on to escape the consequences of his own aggression.

This time the blow goes home. It crashes against Burns's jaw with bone-crunching force. The champion of the world is lifted off his feet. In the sudden silence the thwack of his head against the floor of the ring can be heard. Then there is a roar, the roar of the whole white world that realizes in a flash, in a moment, that the end of its age of supremacy is at hand.

The roar is cut off. As if by magic the time-keeper's count is suddenly heard—"Three . . . four . . . five . . . six . . . seven . . . eight . . .' Burns is on his feet again. Afterwards he claims that it is while the referee is ordering them to break and is actually holding his left glove to pull them apart that the blow goes home. He also claims, against the evidence of most of the experts' ears, that he is up at the count of *four*.

Not that it matters much. He is up: that is the main thing. He covers up, but he goes forward. Johnson clubs him with a right hook to the jaw that would have stunned a steer. Burns reels, rolls away from the next punch, comes in again and sends over a right of his own that jerks back the Negro's head as if his neck must snap. Johnson's smile grows wider than ever. 'Poor little Tommy,' he murmurs kindly, 'did someone kid you you were a fighter?' Burns bundles in again: Johnson knocks up six blows in a row, raining his terrific blocking hits against Burns's biceps as the punches sing through the air.

The bell rings and the men go back to their corners: Johnson like a high-stepping dancer in a night club; Burns slowly and thoughtfully. Pat O'Keefe works furiously on the champion, gesticulating as he fits him to continue in good shape.

As soon as the second round starts, Johnson, through his grinning teeth, invites Burns to come in and swap punches, then whirls over an invisibly fast right swing that drops the champion in his tracks, though he bounces off the floor like india-rubber. As they clinch Burns shouts to McIntosh, 'He's holding, ref.' But it is bluff. It is Burns who is holding for dear life.

Burns is ready to bluff Johnson as well as the referee. Short of breath as he is, he somehow finds it possible to talk to his enemy. 'Why don't you break, nigger? Why don't you come in and fight like a white man?' As he says it, he grips his man—but in vain. Johnson has his measure and is rattling home a tattoo of punches to the stomach. This is close-quarters work such as Pat O'Keefe never dreamed of.

Once in a while Burns skips clear. His legs are his allies still: not for nothing was he a swift and manœuvrable lacrosse player as a boy.

Johnson's tongue is as lively as Burns's legs. 'Come on, you yellow cur. I'm here to fight, not to talk. Come on and fight—if you've got the guts!'

Burns tries to assure himself that Johnson isn't happy. Maybe he is talking to himself as a kid whistles in the dark.

But at the round's end the men at the ringside who have been lucky enough to get their money on Burns have long and anxious faces. Even after the first round they had somehow managed to cheer themselves up by repeating old Fitz's dictum: 'The bigger they come, the harder they fall.' Somehow it sounds pretty hollow now.

The third round gives these brave backers a breathing space. Burns seems to have been given good advice in his corner. He doesn't try to carry the fight to the Negro. He tucks his chin into his left shoulder; he crouches, so that it is almost impossible for Johnson to land a long, lashing blow through the long arms that wrap up the target for the assault. When Johnson taunts him as a back-pedalling world's champion coward he keeps his head, and he keeps it well covered. When Johnson comes prancing in, he burrows under his guard and hammers him with short-arm blows that are satisfactorily heavy. Once he pops up out of his burrow and shoots a straight right to the jaw. Just before the bell Johnson wraps a left swing around his kidneys. For once, the round is halved.

It is one of few. Johnson is at his best in the fourth round, both verbally and with his fists. As Burns comes in, he greets him with a mocking smile and begins to chatter. 'Come and get it, little Tommy. Come and get it! Who told you I was yellow? You're *white*, dead scared white—white as the flag of surrender. You like to eat leather? Have two helpings, you filthy white cur, you.' And both left and right are shot over into the square Napoleonic face. One of Burns's eyes is swelling already and the blood is gushing from the cut lips that do their best to keep up with Johnson's invective.

At the round's end they clinch and McIntosh yells to them to break. They don't break, and he tries to pull them apart. Johnson is strong enough to heave him across the ring and still have the measure of Burns. The men at the ringside have faces as long as coffee pots now.

Some of the more optimistic cheer up in the fifth round. When the bell sounds Burns leaps out of the corner and finds Johnson with his guard down. The left hook lands crashingly in Johnson's face, not on the jaw, not where it can do any good—but still it lands, and hard enough for Johnson to spit forth a little stream of blood.

'See, Tommy? The same colour as a white man's blood. The same colour as a yellow fella's blood . . .' And the long stabbing left lead proves that he is speaking the truth. But Burns comes back. He has yet to win a round, he has yet to look as if he *could* win a round; but he is not done with yet. He comes in during the final minute, gets the inside position and hammers away at Johnson's body. Half a dozen trip-hammer blows crunch against the ribs.

The bell goes at last and Burns almost swaggers back to Pat O'Keefe in his corner. He has taken a round at last—or at least many spectators (but not Jack London) believe he has taken a round. The pent-up joy of twenty thousand white men (less the two ladies and a handful of Negroes) is beautiful to hear. The thunderous cheers are like a message on the bush telegraph to the forty thousand standing in the baking sunshine outside. From lip to lip the report goes; *Burns has won the fifth. The fight is swinging the white man's way at last. There's nothing to worry about after all.* The message is flashed by telegraph to the lamplit reporters' room in Calcutta—somebody opens a bottle of Scotch and finds some soda water that is no more than lukewarm in case it may really be an occasion for celebration.

But the boys around Darlinghurst haven't time to celebrate. The bush telegraph outside the Stadium brings the message up the steep hill to King's Cross that Johnson was laughing in Burns's face as he took that plastering in the ribs and now he comes out for the sixth round with the glare of vengeance in vicious unblinking eyes. He slinks in, swift and silent as a puma, and he purrs as he rocks Burns's head back with that left that is like a well-oiled piston in its steel thrust. Another left—for the days of humiliation when his mother wasn't allowed to share a tram-car with white tramps in Texas! A right like a blow from a bludgeon for being pushed off the streets into the gutter by some white aristocrat of the Chicago Stock-yard! A smash in the torn mouth to drown the sneers and gibes of years in the blood of the very man who had uttered them! A one-two from arms like ramrods—in memory of the slaves in his ancestry who had been flogged raw to amuse the white men and their families on the long Sabbath evenings.

And all the time now, with every blow, the yet unkinder lash of his tongue. Then, suddenly—in the middle of the sixth round—Johnson contrives to lay the supreme insult like a drench of salt upon poor Tommy's wounds. He stands in the middle of the ring, drops his gloves and with his sneering smile begs Tommy to hit him. 'Hit me again, Tommy! Go on—harder this time!' he jeers. Then, while strangled grief can be heard from the crowd he has gestured to join in the laugh, he grips Burns by the left shoulder—and pulls him down into that executioner's slash of an uppercut, delivered with the feet flat on the ground—the gigantic body bending into the stroke.

Burns's eye is swelling now—it is ten to one Pat O'Keefe will have to lance it and suck the blood out. Johnson tenderly frames the target; plants punches above and below it—'So sorry, Tommy, old boy,'—and then shoots that long left out straight at the bull's eye, a blow so powerful that it might have been a jolt from an uprooted telegraph pole. When Burns staggers in to close quarters, Johnson sinks quick fists into the almost skinned stomach, and rolling his eye to the ringside asks: 'Didn't they tell us this boy was an in-fighter?'

No purpose in the world is served by continuing the fight beyond this point—no purpose, at least, in the white world. It has been proved now beyond doubt that Johnson is the master of the champion of the world. Even the betting boys acknowledge it, those most sentimental of experts who had cheered themselves up before the first gong by insisting that Burns was the better bet for the fight. Even they are now shouting Johnson at 2–1 on, and finding no white patriots prepared to support the Caucasian race.

Yet the fight has to go on, because Johnson wills it so. Johnson has not yet taken the toll he demands of the white man. Hell is not too hot nor eternity too long for the punishment he plans to mete out to Tommy Burns. Before he is through with him, that champion of the world will pray for mercy and wish with all his cracking heart that he had remained plain Mr Noah Brusso, never quitting the obscurity of the Canadian outback.

In the eighth round Johnson remembers again Burns's taunts, repeated across America, shouted over France and England and Australia, that his challenger has a yellow streak. 'Tommy—where's my yellow streak?' he wants to know. 'Come and show the customers just where it is.' And the gallant Burns is still able to mouth back insults at his tormentor through the red tatters of his lips.

The pattern of the fight is unvaried now. There remains but one incident to vary the long, terrible saga of the Negro's ascendancy. Johnson is so much at his ease at this stage that he is able to glance around at leisure to observe how the spectators are enjoying his show. Far away, perched on a wall on the edge of the arena, he spots a Negro boy who is really entering into the spirit of the fight. Whenever Jack plunges out his left, the boy flashes out a left lead too. When Jack swings his right, the kid swings his—he is fighting his hero's fight with him, blow for blow. Johnson begins to watch his fan more closely than he bothers to watch Burns. In the twelfth round, indeed, he is so engrossed in the boy's performance that he almost walks into a gigantic swing into which Burns puts all his final, despairing strength. But as Burns telegraphs the blow, Johnson ducks almost to the floor. When he straightens up, he looks for his imitator; and he is not there. He has ducked even as Johnson has ducked—and fallen off the wall. None at the ringside can understand Johnson's cackle of laughter as the twelfth round wears to its close.

There is not much left of Burns's time of agony, or of Burns's tenure of the championship of the world. As the thirteenth round ends, the police at the ringside begin to show signs of interest in the proceedings. It has occurred to them that it will be awkward from their point of view if Burns actually drops dead in the ring. They send Hugh McIntosh over to ask Burns how he is feeling. He comes back with the astonishing report that the champion is feeling fine and would be obliged if the referee would tell the police to mind their own damn business.

Outwardly Burns bears several signs of the merciless hammering he has received. His eyes are swollen and discoloured, his mouth is cut to ribbons, his jaw is horribly swollen and believed (incorrectly as it turns out) to be broken. The white man always declared that Johnson had two broken ribs to defend at this stage of the fight, but it is doubtful whether anyone else would agree with him. The Negro seems to be unmarked and breathing as easily as in the first round.

The bell rings for the fourteenth round. The two men meet in the centre of the ring and Johnson immediately drives his man before him with jabs that land at will. When Burns blindly clutches him, he breaks the clinch by hurling little Tommy from him; as he totters back, unleashing that all but decapitating right uppercut. Burns thuds to the ground flat as a starfish. Immediately there is an uproar. The Sydney-siders have lost their bets, their racial pride, their faith in God—but not their humanity. They hurl cries at the referee, urging him to stop the fight, to save Burns's life. As the boxer totters to his feet, the police inspector leaves his seat by the ring-side and climbs through the ropes. He goes up to the referee and can be seen gesturing—his voice is inaudible against the din. And now Hugh McIntosh raises his right hand. His outstretched finger points to Johnson. For the first time in history a Negro is heavyweight champion of the world.

Johnson has won fairly and squarely, even if it is true he has shown a brutality perhaps never surpassed in the history of the ring in humiliating and torturing his man, instead of contenting himself with merely knocking him senseless.

For Burns the fourteenth round at Rushcutters Bay is the end of the most brilliant chapter in his life. He is given the £6,000 he has earned by unflinching courage, and before he leaves Australia has lost the lot at trotting meetings.

He retired in 1918, but as a tubby middle-aged man he attempted a come-back and was good enough at least to stay with the British champion, Joe Beckett, for seven rounds. He was not, even by modern standards, an outstanding title-holder. He lacked Corbett's elegances of style and the prodigious hitting power of the titanic Jeffries. He was quick, clever, a personality in his own right, but he had as strong a will as any business man with a success story behind him. He always affected to believe that he had an excellent chance of beating Johnson but for the police's craven action in bringing the bout to a halt. He was prepared to admit that he might have been just behind on points, but this, he explained, was due to the risks he was compelled to take to force the Negro to box him at long range. In fact, of course, no man ever lost a fight by a wider margin.

Had Burns kept to the light-heavyweight limit, which was indeed his class, he would have been a hard man to depose; but in his age hardly anybody knew or cared who was the cruiser-weight champion and there were certainly no big purses to be won in championship fights in that division. In his later years Burns took Holy Orders like Bendigo before him and many another champion in his wake.

The end of a brilliant chapter for Burns, the beginning of a life of glory for John Arthur Johnson! He had lived humbly, he had gone hungry, he had been turned out into the snow, he had waited on the mat till the great men of the National Sporting Club could find time to deign to take notice of him. Now it was all going to be different. It was his turn to push cheap white trash off the sidewalks, to entertain the most voluptuous women to champagne and caviare, to ride in gold-plated cars, to flash a gold-toothed smile at the world. He wasn't going to let that turn go by—no sir, not by all the memories of the shabby little house above the Galveston dockyard.

Negroes all the world over would be hailing him as the deliverer and uplifter of their persecuted race. He had avenged Molyneux from Virginia who had gone to England to fight Tom Cribb a hundred years before, and been robbed of the championship when Cribb's supporters broke one of his fingers; and after that, Cribb's second, with his man knocked out in his corner, had stopped the bout to have investigated his false claim that the Negro was fighting with lead in his fists. He had avenged poor Peter Jackson, who had been good enough to slash down Slavin and give Corbett the hardest battle he ever had in his life, but against whom Sullivan had drawn his inexorable colour line. He had avenged them all. All the Negroes who had gone hungry and been spurned and treated like animals while the white men walked the earth like gods.

He was the best man in the world—John Arthur Johnson, a Negro! Now he was going to show them the deference due to the best man in the world.

What he showed them was the strut, the swagger, the cake-walk. None can have felt surprise that the dog let off the leash should have bared his teeth in the first flush of freedom. The first result of his victory was an offer of a three months' tour of the American variety theatres at £350 a week. The money was worth picking up, and Jack enjoyed every minute of peacocking down-stage, especially while there were glorious women in the boxes. Moreover he was good on the stage: witty, and endowed with a presence, while his famous sense of timing was evident as in the ring itself.

But in the meanwhile his victory and the idolizing of Australian crowds had set the white race simmering. Because Johnson had beaten Burns there were innocent Negroes lynched and accorded the honours of necktie parties in the southern states; there were battles to the death around Harlem; there were razors flashing in the cobbled streets of New Orleans and in the mean alleys behind the Chicago stockyards.

Good enough! But what was being done about wiping the memory of Johnson off the face of God's green earth? The white man had heard the tally-ho at the covert-side: the hunt was up. In no gymnasium from Santiago to Perth was a white boy with a punch allowed to escape without further trials of strength being arranged for him. The rough boys of the Marseilles dockyards, the tigers of Woolloomooloo and the muscle-bound back-woodsmen on Lake Superior—all were watched and weighed in the balance, and found wanting.

Throughout the white world the great tip, the tip that must bring results, still seemed to be the message written by Jack London with the horror of the Sydney fight still starkly fresh before him. 'The fight!' he had written in the columns of the *New York Herald*. 'There was no fight! No American massacre could compare to the hopeless slaughter that took place in the Sydney Stadium. The fight, if fight it must be called, was like that between a pigmy and a colossus. It had all the seeming of a playful Ethiopian at loggerheads with a small white man—of a grown man cuffing a naughty child—of a monologue by Johnson who made a noise with his fist like a lullaby, tucking Burns into a crib—of a funeral, with Burns for the late deceased, Johnson for the undertaker, grave-digger and sexton, all in one. . . . So far as damage was concerned, Burns never landed a blow. He never fazed the black man. It was not Burns's fault however. He tried every moment throughout the fight, except when he was groggy. It was hopeless, preposterous, heroic! He was a glutton for punishment as he bored in all the time, but a dewdrop had more chance than he with the giant Texan.'

And so to the bugle call at the end. 'But one thing now remains. Jim Jeffries must now emerge from his alfalfa farm and remove that golden smile from Jack Johnson's face.

'Jeff, it's up to you. The White Man must be rescued.'

So no doubt he must be. But Jeffries perhaps had a right to wonder why it was up to him. The world was urging him back into the ring, and the New Year bells had just rung in the year 1909. It was ten years since he had won the title from Fitzsimmons. It was nine years since (having been outboxed by Jim Corbett for twenty-three of the twenty-five rounds they fought) he beat the boxing phenomenon of the age for the first time. How he had revelled in that victory, and in its repetition—over ten rounds—three years later!

To have beaten Corbett was the most delicious moment in Jeffries' life; almost a moment of fantasy, of wish-fulfilment, for when he was a young fellow he had called at Corbett's quarters, touched his forelock and asked for a job as a sparring partner—and been given one as a floor-sweeper.

They could say what they liked about Jeffries, but he had beaten Ruby Robert and Gentleman Jim and Peter Jackson and Tom Sharkey, and no one had beaten him: no one in the world. He had finished fighting in 1903—six years ago. He had enjoyed life since. One of the newspaper writers had talked about his stomach being well-lined with cocktails. If it was true, hadn't he deserved them?

But Jack London's words dinned in his ears and letters began to come in from all over the world, and everyone he had a drink with would wring his hand and say: 'Proud to shake the fist that's going to knock out Jack Johnson. When's it going to be, Jeff?'

And on top of all that, he loathed Johnson. He didn't like Negroes at the best of times, but of all Negroes he hated Johnson worst. For years now he had said every brutal thing he could think of to insult and degrade the man. He had been told by a friend, and it was probably the truest word ever spoken, that he was the only man alive Johnson was really eager to fight so that he could ram those taunts and insults down his throat to see if they mixed well with the cocktails. He had been told, too, that Johnson had scornfully declared that for years he had known he had Jim Jeffries beaten—ever since he had licked his brother Jack in five rounds in Oakland, California, way back in 1902. According to Johnson this blot on the family escutcheon took all the fight out of Jim Jeffries, once and for all.

On every ground, Jim Jeffries must have hoped that he wouldn't have to return to the ring he had quitted majestically as Tamburlaine so long ago. And perhaps, after all, he wouldn't. To begin with, Johnson seemed quite happy doing his song and dance act around the halls. To go on with, there were plenty of managers with youngsters who believed that they had the next world's champion—

and, of course, a white man at that—right there in their hands. It was quite unnecessary to dig out good old Jeff from his well-earned retirement: 'Just let my boy redeem the White Race instead.'

So it was that Jeffries' ordeal was postponed, until after Johnson had finished his barn-storming tour and taken toll of the cream of the younger talent. It wasn't until July 1910 that Jeffries was called upon to crawl through the ropes once more: six years after he had quit the ring, as he hoped, for good.

When Jim Jeffries made his attempt at a come-back, it was, of course, far too late in the day for him to cherish serious hopes of success. When the youngsters were given their chances it was, generally speaking, far too early; though it would be true to say that few of them would have had any chance against Johnson at any stage of their careers.

And at this point, with the victory over Burns behind him and the crucial contest with Jeffries still over the horizon, it is important to take stock of Jack Johnson, the man and the fighter. We left him intoxicated with triumph, unable to take his oats, blatantly boorish in the first flush of freedom from want and from the world's contempt or neglect.

What would he do?

He immediately did the three worst things he could possibly have done. First, he threw off Sam Fitzpatrick, his manager, the man who had brought him from obscurity to his present eminence; the man whose position and influence alone had been able to raise the money to chase Burns from America to England, across France, to Australia, and finally into the ring at Rushcutters Bay. What did he want with Sam Fitzpatrick any more, asked Johnson. He had £5,000 in his pocket, a contract for his vaudeville tour, the world's title shining over his head like a halo, and a fortune in his two fists. To hell with Sam Fitzpatrick! This breach with his best ally cost Johnson the respect of any influential supporters he might ever have had or hoped to win in the United States.

His second act of folly was to repudiate his contract to fight Langford at the National Sporting Club in London. There was the letter, in black and white, promising to appear in the ring on a date in February 1909. Johnson forfeited the respect of all English well-wishers when he retorted to the secretary, without whose aid he would never have been able to reach Australia, that this was a document for which Fitzpatrick was responsible and which he himself did not regard as binding.

Thirdly, he attached to himself Belle Schreiber, a white woman, with whom he was to travel around America: an act of folly for which he was to pay heavily five years later.

Hated, despised by men of probity and standing who had previously accorded him the bitter compliment of completely ignoring his existence, Johnson found himself fawned on and idolized by every vicious type the prize ring attracts. He revelled in their admiration. He lapped it up as a starving man will guzzle a banquet from every dish set before him: you must not expect from him the dainty discrimination of a gourmet.

So when the vaudeville tour came to an end and Johnson was ready for the ring again, he took his responsibilities to the public and to his new great position lightly indeed. He had no illusion as to the quality of the opposition he was asked to tackle. 'Cheap white trash,' he crowed. 'Not fit to wipe my knuckles on.' Feeble enough, indeed, for him to settle down to a steady training diet of whole roast chickens, champagne and cigars.

They brought the sacrificial victims up to the altar, and hoped that perhaps the gross, indolent Johnson might be caught napping, and so undone. Philadelphia Jack O'Brien who got the first cut at the title-holder must have wished with all his heart that his Quaker home-town had been prepared to recognize boxing so that the referee could give a verdict at the end of that six-round no-decision bout in which he had clearly out-pointed the champion. But Johnson knew that O'Brien couldn't punch his way out of a paper bag and hadn't bothered to train before going through the old routine. At the end of that travesty of a contest, which we have already mentioned, he had the impudence to grin at the customers, as if inviting them to agree with him that it was amazing how little you could get for your money.

VII

++

So, AFTER ALL, the nearest thing anyone could find to a White Hope to do the job of 'whacking the nigger', as stipulated by the school of Jack London, was Jim Jeffries, the retired champion. Jeffries had been one of the grandest fighters of an heroic age. He had spent seven years in the ring (before returning for this single fight in 1910), and for four of those seven years he was world's champion. He learned much of the technique of the game from Tommy Ryan, a famous middleweight of the day who taught him to crouch, which kept him out of the way of Fitzsimmons' body-punching in one of the most important contests of his career.

Jeffries was undefeated before his come-back to meet Johnson. He had been held to draws by Gus Ruhlin and Joe Choynski, but had twice knocked out Fitzsimmons, twice beaten Sharkey, and twice defeated Corbett. His first defeat of Corbett, on the war path to win his second title, was fortunate indeed. For fifteen rounds the bout was like an exhibition between master and pupil, and though much of the steam went out of Corbett at this stage, he was still easily on top on points when knocked out, despite Jeffries' skilful use of the left hook to the body which was the only punch his opponent found hard to evade.

But Jeffries was a big man and a big champion, no mere conjuror who had fluked his way to the title. His crouch might have disgusted the old masters, Figg and Cribb and even Mace; but his straight left was the grandest punch the ring knew between Fitzsimmons' wallop to the solar plexus and Dempsey's right jab. He was a giant—the old boiler-maker. When he first beat Fitzsimmons he was fifty-five pounds the heavier man. Though he was nine years older than Corbett, the brilliant boxer (first of a new school of scientific performers) had affected to consider him small beer indeed. The marvellous straight left, the cunning crouch, and the patient readiness to take punishment till the reddened ring was slippery and his opponent exhausted with the work of butchery—these qualities stood to his credit.

When he retired in 1904 he was unapproached, and he was

allowed, as we know, to hand over his championship to be fought for by Marvin Hart (who, you will remember, had once beaten an inexperienced Johnson) and Jack Root, the first cruiser-weight title holder. Now, six years later and six years too late, he came back. His speed had evaporated. The champion's gift of cramming on full sail when the wind of destiny blew—that was gone too. Only the ox-like strength was there: the great, grunting, lumpish blood-and-sinew which would get whacked from Reno to Christmas time and still come up for more.

A new man came out of the West to stage the Johnson-Jeffries fight. And yet Tex Rickard, tough as a cowboy in a silent film, wasn't quite a new boy. He had made a name for himself by staging the first Gans-Nelson contest at Goldfield, Nevada. Now he took a chance and pitted the most unpopular man in the white world against the Homeric hero Jack London had hailed as the destined restorer of its dynastic supremacy. Rickard revelled in the situation. He was a gambler to the tips of his horny fingers. He chuckled as he saw the 42,000, enemies to their bared teeth, who had come to see Johnson beaten, or better still lynched. The Negro had done his bit to add to the electricity in the atmosphere by publicly stating that he was in the ring to beat Jeffries because his ambition was to make the white man kow-tow to him.

Rickard laughed when he heard the bragging words. This was the fight game as he knew and loved it. He had his own way of checking the crowd: he made every bravo among them (and most of those known to be wanted by the police in every State of the Union were present) check his gun or his knife at the cloakroom before going to his seat. Then he counted the takings before climbing into the ring to referee the fight; and for once a delighted gleam shone in the blue marble eyes of that astute poker player. For the first time in the history of boxing more than a quarter of a million dollars had been taken at the turnstiles.

Now all that remained was to offer the crowd of the century a fight they would never forget. Rickard experienced a fleeting hope that Johnson was in perfect shape. His friend Hugh D. McIntosh had had a curious story to tell him. He had called on Johnson at his training quarters a week or two back and found a bloated, curiously grey-skinned fellow lazily cuffing a punch-ball whenever the sun was under the yard-arm. McIntosh had in his belt most of the £26,000 he had made out of promoting the Johnson-Burns fight, every penny of which he had brought to America to bet on the champion. What he saw made him wonder whether he oughtn't to hedge his investment. He put the point to Johnson.

'Don't you worry at all, Mr Mac. I'm going to be fit as a black panther on the day. The way I am now is intentional—to lengthen the odds. Put every penny on me you've got to spend.'

McIntosh knew his man, and was impressed. There remained the question of Jack's curious greyish colour. Diffidently, McIntosh raised the question—anyway, it probably in no way affected Jack's chances against Jeffries.

'Think nothing of it, Mr Mac. I'm *sunburned*, that's all. Just put every penny you've got on me for this fight.' Though Johnson was nearly two stone overweight and still inclined to postpone the hardships of training, Hugh D. McIntosh had taken his advice.

And so to Reno on 4 July 1910. The crowd were thin-lipped, narrow-eyed, behind Jeffries almost to a man. They hadn't come to see a fight; they had come to witness an execution. They had been told by all the boxing writers that Jeffries was certain to win, and they lowered at Johnson, or spat brutal words towards his corner. They were 42,000 to one before ever the bell went for the first round. The most popular tune the band played that day was 'All Coons Look Alike to Me'.

The bravest man at Reno was the champion. He was as scornful of the mob as he was of Jeffries. As he stood in his corner, he looked around him for the bitterest enemy he could find in the crowd. Corbett would do. The old champion was there in Jeffries' corner. Jack waved to him as David might have waved to Jonathan. He flashed the golden smile at him. Corbett's face was of stone. None of the boys in big Jim's corner would give him a smile—not Sam Berger, Joe Choynski or Farmer Burns, or Abe Attell, 'The Dancing Master', who had won the world's featherweight championship when he knocked out Brooklyn Tommy Sullivan a couple of years before. In Johnson's own corner were Kid Cotton, Billy Delaney, Tom Flannigan, Barney Furey and Frank Sutton. Stanley Ketchel was Johnson's time-keeper; Rickard himself the referee.

The two men had entered the great open-air arena at two-thirty; there had been no preliminary contests. This was the fight of the day, of the century; nothing else counted or could be stomached.

From the first bell there was never any doubt as to who was going to win. Jeffries had been blatantly confident until then, but as soon as action was asked of him, his lack of belief in himself was clearly exhibited. As for Johnson, he was at the peak of his form, quicker

on his feet than ever before, swaying out of reach of Jeffries' ponderous left leads, dancing back to land his own counter-punches at
will. Once or twice they came to close-quarters where it had been
believed that Jeffries would be particularly effective, and once again
it was Johnson who was top dog. There was a complete absence of
the furious charges that had swept champions before old Jeff in the
past. He did no more than shuffle around with a wary expression in
the eye that had been guaranteed to flash lightnings.

For four rounds Johnson toyed with him, springing in like a beast
to the kill, then—his face split open in a smile—gently flicking the
great puffy face with his glove, and dancing away out of range again.
By the fifth round it was clear to all that the Negro was on top and
could end the fight whenever his sense of sadistic fun was satisfied.

But Jack was in no hurry. During the eighth round he had
found a new amusement: a little back-chat with acquaintances
round the ringside who had spent the sixty-day training period
before the fight telling the world that Jeff was a certain winner. At
last Jeffries lost all restraint and came wading in to aim a flurry of
punches at the Negro's ribs. The crowd—the silent, resentful
crowd—sat up, moved forward on its haunches, stood on tiptoe, and
at last began to cheer in a roar of acclamation. But the surge of sound
ebbed away when it was seen with what consummate ease Johnson
rode the storm of punches, taking them on gloves and forearm,
slithering away when Jeff came hurtling into a corner, turning to
pick his man off with a left that flipped his head back like the lid on a
biscuit tin. Then he spotted Corbett, glum and hopeless below the
ropes behind Jeffries' back. 'Hello there, Jim! Welcome to the
village! Did you happen to notice that little left-hander there? And
how about this one?' And over went a right hook under which
Jeffries reeled in stricken ineptitude.

There were so many old friends at the ringside! 'Ah there,
Farmer! Ever see a champ eat leather? You watch Jeff. He just
loves to swallow mouthfuls all day long. Don't you, Champ?' And
thud, thud, thud into the raw and glistening face went the quick
fists. By the time Jeff had twisted round on his tired old legs to try
to fight back, Jack had skipped to the far corner and was sneering
and chattering behind his gloves to some murderous-looking acquaintance who would have made him guest of honour at a necktie
party without a moment's compunction.

As the round drew to its close, Johnson came boring in boldly, to
clinch and wrestle round the ropes. The old boiler-maker allowed

himself to be pushed around; he hadn't the strength to try to keep his man at bay. 'How do you like this barn dance, Mr Jeffries? Where's your punch, Mr Jeffries? Where's the one that stove in Sharkey's ribs?' Then the bell rang, and Jeff went stumbling to his corner where his seconds worked feverishly on his battered face, while Gentleman Jim Corbett gesticulated as he poured down on the head sunken on the heaving chest a stream of advice and inspiration intended to swing the tide of battle at the eleventh hour. As the miracle-workers went about their frantic business in Jeff's corner, Jack lolled at ease in his chair, waving and calling out to his most embittered enemies at the ring-side. He had hardly worked up a healthy sweat. He looked as if he were good to fight another forty rounds.

All through the ninth round Johnson's footwork was as nimble and point-device as a polo pony's. When Jeff rushed him into a corner, he could pivot on the big toes and tuck home a couple of crunching body blows, before coming up like a jack-in-the-box at the other side of the ring. But Jack wasn't fighting on the run now. Often he stood his ground and stopped Jeff charging like a wounded buffalo, with a ringing left hand that closed the white man's eyes before the round was out. Each time this classic blow clove Jeff's feeble defences, Johnson would flash his smile to Hugh McIntosh and Tommy Burns, sitting together at the ringside. 'So they said I couldn't punch,' he crowed. 'There's one I forgot to show you in Sydney.'

The last puff of steam was gone from Jeff now. He had fought on long after the light of hope had been quenched in the despairing dream that a chance punch might somehow catch Johnson off his balance. But now, even if the punch were thrown, even if Johnson plunged head on into it, he could hardly hope that it would swing the fight. He tottered around the ring, he tottered to his corner. He could hardly see. The great Pacific that he had known æons ago when he had gone fishing with his dad as a boy, was pouring through his broken head with a mounting roar.

His seconds pulled him back into his corner. He heard Corbett's eternal voice mouthing away all the platitudes about the honour of the White Race. Where he was, there wasn't any White Race; there was just the roar of the sea and a mocking smile and heavy jolts of pain that tore at his raw and twitching nerves. He knew the end was very near now.

He heard someone say it was the fourteenth round and tried to remember how many rounds there were in a fight. He moved in a nightmare into the corner of the ring, and Johnson, laughing lightly, met him with a crashing left hand like a jolting battering-ram. He grabbed the Negro and clung to him. Johnson flung him off and rammed in two short-arm blows on the bloated, bloody eyelids; then sprang apart and rained in long whiplash punches. But old Jeff had a sort of hopeless indestructibility about him that afternoon. He still went shambling forward, like some sort of blundering sleep-walker trying to pad his way home. Once or twice he actually hit Johnson with that famous left, which now had only the effect of widening the Negro's smile.

Halfway through the round Johnson met the advancing Jeffries with three terrific straight lefts which set his head rocking on his shoulders. 'How do you feel, Jim?' he asked solicitously as they clinched. Perhaps the cool cynicism of the sneer woke some last flicker of spark in Jeffries. At all events, he threw everything into a final despairing effort. He waded into the attack, and waded is the word, for he was shrunk at the knees like a man half-surrendering to lethargy. He went in with all guns firing, but there was so little powder behind the shells.

Suddenly the avuncular smile was brushed off Johnson's face. There was no longer the dancing look of merriment in the eyes. The face was the cruel mask of a puma closing in on his prey. He slung Jeffries back across the ring with a huge left swing, and chased him from corner to corner contemptuously bashing home the same artless blow as if to emphasize how completely the wobbling white giant was at his mercy.

Then Johnson stood off, shook his bald poll from side to side, breathed deeply, and brought a bone-crushing left and right to the jaw. Jeffries' eyes glazed, almost between punches. He spread his big gloves before him feebly as a child might, to ward off the witch in a story. Then slowly, hopelessly, with the look of a factory chimney crumpling, big Jim Jeffries reeled backward, sank into the ropes, lay spreadeagled across the floor. Never before had Jeffries been knocked off his feet. It wasn't the end of the fight, but it was something yet more final and more terrible; the end of a reputation. The end of a legend.

Nor was the end of a fight long delayed. The beaten figure lolling over the ropes on to the floor was heaved upright from outside the ring by one of his seconds. As his gloves left the floor Johnson sprang in, but Rickard the referee made a movement as if to jump in between the fighters—then he hesitated, and as Jeffries staggered across the ring Johnson hooked him ruthlessly on the side of his head. Jeffries slumped forward on his face, and as the count began the crowd started to leave their seats and poured forward to surround the ringside. Their shouts drowned the count—'Stop it! Stop the fight! Don't let him be knocked out!' The tears were streaming down many hickory faces swarming up to the ropes.

But in the dazed and uncomprehending Jeffries, the fighting instinct flickered yet. He crawled off the floor with a second of the count to go. Once again Johnson sprang at him, and Jeffries somehow found the strength to clinch desperately before the great right swing could be launched. But his strength had ebbed away now. Johnson shook him off contemptuously, and as he did so, Sam Berger, Jeffries' chief second, clambered up to the ropes and threw in the sponge in recognition of defeat. Rickard's back was towards Berger, however, and he did not see the token of surrender until after Johnson had bashed home his last full-blooded right of the contest to lay Jeffries helpless at his feet. The fight was over: there was no beating the count this time. Jeffries was on his knees like a slave in the train of his master when the tenth second was tolled out.

Johnson's victory was the completest thing the glove game ever knew, yet so determined were the supporters of the Aryan race to refuse to believe in the Negro's supremacy that they had a pre-fabricated explanation ready for the emergency: Jeff had been 'got at' with a draught of poisoned tea. The story did not win the support of many floating voters. The plain fact was that Johnson had outclassed Jeffries throughout the contest, had played with him as a cat plays with a hypnotized mouse, and finally, having become serious about his executioner's job, had chopped him down with a savage relish.

The real question that remained was—how good was Johnson now? No one could answer that one with glib confidence. Assuming that Corbett was the first of the scientific boxers, few would deny at this period that Johnson eclipsed Corbett in skill or in subtlety as a counter-puncher. Two of his finest punches won the respectful admiration of those who regarded Peter Jackson as the G.O.M. of the glove game. The first of these was the straight left, shot out quiveringly fast and amazingly effective from his extraordinary ability to re-direct it in mid-air. 'You covered up your point,' said a sparring-partner, 'and that wicked punch which you saw whizzing along for you a foot away, came through to land over your heart.'

The straight left lead was one of Johnson's most devastating blows when it was aimed at the throat, and it was hardly less conclusive when employed as a defensive weapon against the biceps of an opponent who was leading to him. But perhaps the most penetrating shot in Johnson's armour was still his right uppercut. He continued to whip it home without change of stance—swung short and sharp to the chin, with a wiggle from the hips which somehow added to the momentum. A real pendulum punch, made perfect by the split-second slipping of the head inside the enemy's left lead.

But after the Jeffries' fight, the champion's defensive skill was his greatest strength. For a big man, he was as delicate in his movements as a kitten with a toy. He boxed on his toes, swayed and shifted as tirelessly and neatly as a featherweight, and enjoyed establishing his moral superiority in a contest before setting the seal of victory on his performance. After he had made his opponent appear as unsubtle as a clown, he would gradually grind him down and then put him away conclusively at his own convenience.

VIII

MOST OF THE MISFORTUNES of Jack Johnson's life were crowded into the years that followed the victory over Jeffries on 4 July 1910, though his troubles began surely enough when he took the world's title from Burns. Less than a year after the Jeffries match, Johnson married Etta Duryea, a white woman of French-American extraction. He first met her, shortly after the Ketchel fight, in the stalls of a New York theatre. One look at Etta was enough to convince Jack that this was the girl he intended to marry. Etta returned the look— and the sentiment.

Within a month Jack had got his wish. His wooing was an affair of diamonds, ermine wraps, gold bracelets and champagne suppers. Etta ran away from her husband to join him. At the Pittsburgh wedding everybody was very grandly dressed indeed, and someone suggested that instead of confetti the guests ought to throw gold dust over the departing couple. It was an old friend who gave the answer: 'Jack's already thrown that into the bride's eyes.'

After the wedding, Jack and Etta set sail for Europe on a theatrical business trip and honeymoon, with the emphasis on the latter.

It was at this stage that the possibility of a contest with Billy Wells was raised in London. After the late Jimmy White and C. B. Cochran had made strenuous efforts to promote the contest, the London County Council stopped the fight by making representations to the Home Secretary, with the result that an injunction was obtained against the free-holders of Earl's Court restraining them from using their building for the staging of such a contest. Public sentiment of the day was outraged at the suggestion of a Black *versus* White fight as a great spectacle: possibly the English were the more distressed because they were well aware of the probable result of such a contest.

There can be no doubt that Jack was, at this time, one of the best-hated Americans alive. His personal life was lived on a scale few wives would appreciate, or care to share. He had a taste for wine, women and the bass viol. He and Etta lived in opulent squalor, not always paying their way. Johnson's landlady at Luxborough House, Northumberland Street, Paddington, threw him off her premises for bad conduct, and then obtained a judgment against him for the destruction of her crockery and furniture. The flat was said to have been left in a miserably dirty condition.

Such a life was too grim for any balanced woman to be asked to share: and Etta Johnson was no balanced woman. After her death (already not very far beyond the horizon) Johnson was to declare that he had twice saved her from suicide: once when she attempted to throw herself to destruction from a London hotel.

If Johnson's private life was shameless and detestable, he was also untrustworthy as a business man. He was engaged to appear at a number of music halls owned by Fred McNaughton, but without a word of warning or explanation broke his contract to pay a trip to Paris, in search, it was said, of pleasure rather than business—though perhaps this might have counted as a mitigating circumstance in his favour. In any event, the English management sued him at the London Sheriff's Court, and obtained judgment for £1,500: the defendant, as was customary on these occasions, not bothering to put in an appearance.

When he *did* appear, he could not complain that he was unappreciated by press and public. In July 1911, he was to be found on exhibition at the Oxford Music Hall, performing on the bass viol, singing 'Baby's Sock is a Blue-bag Now', and finally condescended to spar for a few rounds with a gallant if desperate heavyweight called Monte Cutler. *The Times* was enthusiastic about Johnson's performance. It noted with regret that in his own country he 'passed for a "flash nigger", a type not to be encouraged by those who have to keep ten millions of black men in subjection to the dominant race'. It admired his wit and sportsmanship, and found that, surprisingly enough for one with his background, he retained his faith in humanity—though not when it came to discussing any subject in terms of hard cash. True, he sported rather more gold teeth than were generally worn by men of breeding in the Shires, and enough diamonds to resemble a starry night, but he was, on the whole, 'a far more pleasant person to meet in a room than any of the white champions of complicated nationality whom America exports from time to time to these unwilling shores.'

Of his boxing ability there could be no doubt, though *The Times* gravely diagnosed the vulnerability of the stomach of this 'copper colossus' (reminding one, after all these years, of Sam Langford's retort to the criticism that Negroes didn't like being hit in the midriff—'Sir, nobody *likes* being hit in the stomach'). As for Johnson's defence and speed, these qualities were beyond praise; though Jack failed to draw this critic as he had drawn an Australian expert before the Burns fight, into inquiring into his claim to have been a runner in youth. ('Sprinter or distance runner?' asked the Australian solemnly. 'Sprinter,' Jack admitted coyly, 'I leave long-distance running to little Tommy.')

Yes, *The Times* admitted that Johnson was the paragon of his age. Whatever you might achieve against his stomach, it didn't seem to matter how often, or how hard you hit him on his head: 'a cast-iron lid on flowing shoulder-muscles, like a pepper corn on the Atlantic.'

But though *The Thunderer* purred, the Home Secretary would have none of Johnson. He went home in 1912, to fight Jim Flynn at Las Vegas without fulfilling his ambition of meeting Bombardier Wells in an English ring, to the end of exhibiting to English crowds that their own white heroes were every bit as inferior to the Negro superman as the Americans themselves.

The Jim Flynn fight was grotesque enough. In the first round somebody fired a revolver into the air, and a great cry went up: 'That'll scare the skin off the black beggar.' After that the fight was a dull affair, with Flynn, a Pueblo fireman whose real name was Andrew Haymes, doing much more butting than was strictly conventional in a contest of this description. Johnson won in the ninth round, having added nothing to his reputation. All the same, he showed some courage in knocking Flynn out with a grand right uppercut which dropped the white man face forward onto the floor of the ring. The day before the fight he had received a letter that might have stopped some men from giving of their best. It was brief and to the point. It said *Lie down to-morrow, or we'll string you up*. The signature was K.K.K.

Johnson beat Flynn on 4 July 1912. His victory added to the hatred in which he was held by white Americans, and he may have been telling the truth when he claimed that at this time he was subjected to ceaseless persecution. According to him, it was this unrelenting cruelty which drove Etta to commit suicide two months later.

She hadn't been happy since their return home. The melancholy which had attacked her in London had pursued her to Chicago. The death of her father, who had done everything in his power to smooth her path, had left her with the feeling that she had no real friend outside her own front door. Shortly after their return to the

States, Jack had had forcibly to restrain her from throwing herself under a train.

Then one day they had been entertaining friends at home. When the party broke up, Etta had said: 'You go and see them off at the station, Jack. I'll go and lie down, if you don't mind. I've got one hell of a headache.'

'All right, I won't be long.'

He waved till the train was out of sight, then strolled back through the cool streets, stopping at a drug store to buy a cigar. That was one thing about being a world's champion with no challenger in sight—you could always help yourself to a cigar when you had the mind. He lit up: then suddenly flung the cigar from him. The shop-keeper cried: 'What's wrong, Mr Johnson? That's our best ten-cent cigar,' but Jack wasn't there to hear or explain. He was running, running home like a man with terror in his heart. He couldn't tell why, but he was sure disaster had struck.

Before he reached the house he knew how right his instinct had been. From the end of the street he could see the crowd outside his front door: a silent crowd, straining on tiptoe, their faces grimly eager in the lamplit street. Among them the police threaded their way, pushing a girl aside, shouldering an old man out of the way.

'For the love of Christ, what is it?'

The policeman turned and looked him in the eyes. 'You ought to know. Where've you come from?'

'Tell me—is it my wife?'

The policeman didn't tell him. He seemed more disposed to ask questions than to answer. Jack brushed him aside, barged past two others and was in the bedroom. The doctor by the bedside didn't even bother to tell him to keep quiet; it was too late now for that to be important. The horror of the blood-drenched pillows and the mutilated face that had pressed itself to his a few minutes before, made him stagger like a drunkard. Even then, it was not the end. There was still a flicker of life in the woman, half of whose head was torn away by the revolver shot. She died in hospital that night.

At the inquest Jack told of Etta's previous attempts to commit suicide, and added a footnote which revealed their brief married life in a nightmare light. He, too, he explained, was a victim of suicidal mania—and only his wife had known his secret. *Twice she had pre-vented him from killing himself, as he had twice saved her from self-destruction.*

It was a ghastly picture indeed: the black man and the white

woman, exiled from both their tribes, hating life so intensely that
each had to save the other from the extinction both coveted. And
to save life for what purpose? There was no happiness for the
rescued; no peace in the companionship of the rescuer. For the
survivor there was life, with all its multitudinous agonies and
hatreds and fears and despairs. And for Etta, as Jack saw it, there
was oblivion. Years afterwards he wrote of her that 'she was murdered by the world, by spiteful tongues, by my enemies, by race
hatred. She paid the penalty of my being the heavyweight champion
of the world.' But at the time he probably felt that she was lucky to
get out of life at the cheap cost of everlasting oblivion.

And now the man-hunt against the champion of the world was up
with a vengeance. It cannot be said that Jack was an inconsolable
widower for very long. Two months after the suicide of his wife, he
was in serious trouble with the police over his relations with her
successor; in such serious trouble that it was to overshadow most of
the rest of his life.

With the money he had made out of the Jeffries fight, Jack had
bought a restaurant in Chicago. You could meet anyone in Chicago
in the Café de Champion, under Jack's diamond-framed portrait,
from a politician to a Negro deacon, though the politician was the
likelier. One day when Jack was swaggering through the rooms, helping himself to half a glass from the bottles of gratified customers here
and there, a young girl put her hand on his arm. She was smartly
dressed and pretty. There may have been bigger blue eyes in the
restaurant that night, but if so it was a lucky evening.

'Mr Johnson, do you know what you want? You want a secretary.'

It was an idea. You bet his favourite author, Herbert Spencer, had
had a secretary! Any man that had the job of restoring the Negro
race to its proper pinnacle above the world had a right to a secretary.
'You know five thousand words?' he asked anxiously, 'and all the
long ones?'

She drew a deep breath. She looked more than ever like a picture-
postcard queen when she breathed in deep and her eyes opened
wide. 'Mr Johnson, you're a sophisticated rhetorician, inebriated
with the exuberance of your own verbosity.'

'I am? Is that good?'

'What do you think, Mr Johnson?'

'I think you're hired. Can you type, too?'

Her name was Lucille Cameron, and she came from Minneapolis.
She was white and nineteen years old. He reckoned she could live

out at Jack Curley's place while she held down her job. Jack Curley
was a white man and a friend: there were few in Jack's life that were
either, and none other that was both. There wasn't a nicer fellow
mixed up with the managerial side of the fight game. Curley would
look after Lucille like an uncle, like a great uncle.

But the hounds were on Johnson's tracks now. Not merely was
public opinion against him, the law was ready for him too. Mrs
Cameron-Falconet, Lucille's mother, was determined to get her
daughter out of his clutches. One evening she arrived at his house.
She was sharp-featured, hard-eyed, tense. She put her umbrella
down in the hall as if she were discarding a debating point.

'What's this I hear, Mr Johnson?'

This was the sort of situation that drove him to the nigger talk his
critics liked to emphasize as typical of his social style. 'Not being
cognizant of your audibility, I regret my inabilitude to answer.'

She followed on her formidable course. 'My daughter . . . What,
may I ask, are you doing with my daughter?'

'You may ask. And the answer is in the emphatical negative.'

'What do you mean, Mr Johnson?'

'Nothing, ma'am. Nothing is what I mean. And nothing is what
I am guilty of accomplishing.'

'I must tell you, Mr Johnson, that I have sent for my daughter.
She will be here in a few minutes. I intend to accuse her of her
wickedness to her face. And to *your* face.'

He laughed. Laughing often gave a greater impression of innocence than anything else. 'It will be nice to see her here. I've always
hoped there might be an opportunity of showing her this house.'

'You don't say,' she almost spat. They sat in silence until the
front doorbell rang.

It was Lucille, and a Lucille who had virgin and martyr written all
over her.

'Well, my girl, I want to hear what you've done. I want to hear
what this nigger made you do.'

Lucille said nothing. She eyed her mother as if she were a gibbering maniac on the other side of the street.

'You can't play that game with me. You're under age, and I can
force the truth out of you. And by God, I will. Giving yourself to a
nigger——'

'Who said I did? It's a dirty, filthy lie. The sort of lie only you
would tell.'

'Everyone says it. Everyone in Minneapolis.'

'Everybody in Minneapolis!' Lucille scoffed. 'Everybody in Minneapolis is nobody.'

'You wait till I get you home. You'll find out what the world thinks of a girl who can do that sort of thing with a nigger. Why, an animal wouldn't be worse——'

Jack towered over her. 'Get out! Get out of my house. If you were a man, I'd——'

'Don't you worry what you would do. You worry about what you *will* do! You're going to prison for this. That will be the end of you, you filth.'

Mrs Cameron-Falconet seized Lucille by the arm and pulled her towards the door. 'You try and stop me! She's nineteen, she's under age, you'll get another five years if you lay a finger on me.'

He held open the door. 'I wouldn't lay a finger on you or your daughter for all the gold in the world. The sooner I see the last of you both——' The door slammed in his face.

And now it was the turn of the law. At one stage he was charged with abducting Lucille Cameron. Lucille herself was a witness who was not going to be of any assistance to the Federal officers. She told them: 'I don't care if he is white or black, I love him.' Away in Minneapolis, Mrs Cameron-Falconet declared: 'I'd rather see my daughter dead than marry a black man.'

But that is just what her daughter chose to do. On the third of December 1912, Lucille Cameron married John Johnson at 3344 Wabash Avenue, Chicago. It was a drizzling day when the Reverend H. A. Roberts, an ancient Negro with hair like white wool, knocked on the door. When he came into the parlour, Jack lifted Lucille off his lap, and exclaimed: 'Come on, honey, the preacher's ready.' There were a number of Negroes present, including Jack's mother. But the bride had neither friends nor relations to support her. There were only four white people in the room: Mr Daniels, a saloon-keeper, and his wife; 'Sig' Hart, once a rubber in the gym where Johnson trained; and a lady whom the *Chicago Tribune* tersely described as a 'chemical blonde'.

In the middle of a prayer during the ceremony, a press photographer took a flashlight photograph. Lucille was scared out of her wits. She flung her arms round Jack's neck, and the ceremony was suspended while everyone had a good laugh. After that, the prayer was finished. The highlight of the occasion was when Jack placed a six-carat diamond ring, reported to have cost $2,500, on his bride's finger. After that they kissed, according to the report of those present, 'audibly'.

That was that; Lucille Cameron was Mrs Jack Johnson now. The Negroes present crowded round and told her that she was a fit bride for the superman. She laughed and retorted that Jack wasn't a champion any more. She was the boss in future. 'Isn't that so, Jack?'

'It sure is, honey.'

'Tiny' Johnson gave her daughter-in-law a hug and a kiss, but refused to comment on the wedding. 'Sometimes I say things Jack doesn't approve of, so I'll keep my thoughts to myself.'

A reporter buttonholed Lucille: 'Where's your mother, Mrs Johnson?'

'I don't know and I don't care.'

The reporter hadn't long to wait before the papers told him the answer. In Minneapolis Mrs Cameron-Falconet had swooned when they told her that the wedding was taking place.

Meanwhile in Wabash Avenue the champagne corks were popping, though the atmosphere was not altogether lighthearted. A woman reporter began to ask Jack a number of questions of a searching nature. He didn't like the questions, and said so. The woman reporter asked more, and he liked these less. Finally he turned her out of the house.

It was only a momentary interruption of the festivities. There were more photographs, and when the last of them was taken, Jack took the $2,500 diamond ring off his bride's finger and put it in his waistcoat pocket.

The last question was fired at him as the reporters went out into the drizzle: 'Where are you going for the honeymoon trip?' It was an embarrassing question. The Federal Court held a bond requiring Jack not to leave the State during his case. He replied, with some dignity, that he had thought of taking his wife for a trip round Illinois, in his racing car.

IX

THE CASE AGAINST JACK JOHNSON for abducting Belle Schreiber ended in Judge Carpenter's court at 5.30 p.m. on the evening of 4 June 1913.

In Johnson's early appearances in court in this and other cases there had been scenes of poignant drama, as, for example, when the offer to put up bail of $65,000 was refused, and the champion left court for the cells, handcuffed to Deputy Marshal Edward Northrup. There had been the dramatic moment when a woman witness was discovered in whose house it was said that Johnson had had relations with one girl he was accused of abducting. A fascinating detail was that this important witness had been run to earth in the barn in which she had been hiding for weeks on the corner of Indiana Avenue and Twentieth Street.

Then there was the row about the bondsmen who had gone bail for Johnson. One of them turned out to be a man of straw—a newsboy who had clearly no right to be nominated as a bondsman at all. In fact, it was admitted by the defence that he was to be paid $150 for playing the part.

But the Law finished with Jack at last. On 4 June 1913, Judge Carpenter sentenced him for the crime of which he had been found guilty a month previously—the crime of having transported Belle Schreiber from Pittsburgh to Chicago for immoral purposes. Benjamin Bahrach, Jack's attorney, attempted to bring a motion for a new trial, but this was overruled. Johnson was asked whether he wished to say anything before he was sentenced. He hesitated, and then replied: "No, nothing, your honour." Judge Carpenter then pronounced sentence. He pointed out that there had been cases in which men committed under the Mann Act had been fined and not sent to prison. He considered, however, that Johnson's case was too serious to come within this category. 'This defendant is one of the best-known men of his race, and his example had been far-reaching, and the Court is bound to consider the position he occupied among his people. In view of these facts, this is a case that calls for more than a fine.'

Jack Johnsen, The Famous American Coloured Boxer.

Jack Johnson – A Portrait.

Johnson wins the world title by beating Tommy Burns in Sydney, Australia, in 1908.

Johnson knocks out Stanley Ketchel in California in 1909.

JAMES J. JEFFRIES   JACK JOHNSON

CHRONICLE HAS THE BEST SPORTING PAGES ON THE PACIFIC COAST

1910 advertisement – James J. Jeffries v Jack Johnson.

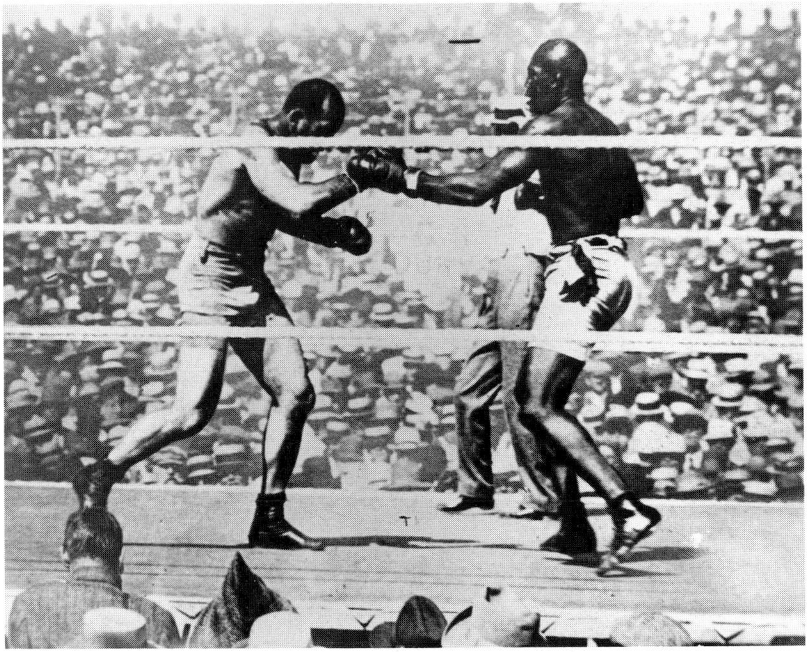

The ageing Jeffries somehow manages to keep going against the virile Johnson.

LEFT In 1911 Jack Johnson married Etta Duryea.

BELOW In his racing car at Brooklands the same year.

RIGHT Johnson with his mother and Lucille Cameron, his third wife, in 1912.

BELOW Mr Harold Davidson, later Rector of Stiffkey, is on the extreme right of this 1911 tea-party.

Jess Willard beating Johnson in Havana, Cuba, in April 1915.

World champion no more! Jack Johnson's seven-year reign is over.

A celebrity in Paris in the thirties – seen here with three French dancers.

Johnson at the age of fifty-three planning to make a barnstorming trip around the US boxing exhibition contests.

The sentence was passed: one year and one day's imprisonment, as well as $1,000 fine.

There was a two weeks' respite before the sentence was due to be carried out, to enable Johnson's attorney to file a bill of error to carry the case to the United States Circuit Court of Appeal. A fortnight's freedom—on bail of $30,000 . . . much could be done in a fortnight.

All his friends told him that he hadn't a chance. When the appeal came on, the conviction would be upheld, and that would be the end of him.

Already he was only a free man on bail of $30,000. His championship would be gone; so would his livelihood. Yet if he slipped out of the United States he would still go on being champion of the world and nobody could touch him.

What was the argument against running away? 'It's you,' he told his mother. 'I don't want to be parted from you. To me, that's worse than prison, it's death.'

His mother stroked his cheek. 'To me, the worst thing in the whole world would be to know you were in prison. And if you stay here, that's where you'll be. Prison! What good are you going to be to me there?'

'Maybe they'll acquit me.'

She groaned. 'They'll never acquit you. You'll go to prison, and that will kill me just as certain as a bullet through the heart.'

He turned to Lucille. 'What do you think?'. .

'You've got to get out, Jack. You've got to fly.'

He stared at his mother. Her hair was grey now. 'But when should I see you again?'

She shrugged her thin little shoulders. 'Who knows? Maybe some politician would do something.'

He said, 'It'll look like running away and leaving you to face the music.'

'It *is* running away. But once you're out of the country there'll be no music to face.'

He got to his feet. His mind was made up now. He'd go—to-morrow, to-night if it was possible. But it wasn't going to be easy. There were still cops around in the street, looking up at the lighted windows as they passed his house. The K.K.K. had ordered him out of town: the law demanded that he stayed and faced his sentence.

Next morning down at the restaurant somebody gave him the big idea. 'Seen Foster's Giants yet?'

'Who the hell are Foster's Giants?'

'It says here in the paper that they're the best baseball team they've sent down from Canada in years. Coloured men, the lot, and they can teach these white boys something about baseball. And look at the photo of this guy. He might be your double.'

That afternoon he was watching the Giants at their workout and soon spotted the man he was looking for. It wasn't difficult to get to meet him in the dressing-room, but it wasn't easy to see why he should agree to his proposition.

'Let me get this straight, brother. You want to change places with me. You want to take my place among our boys when they go back to Canada after to-morrow's game?'

'That's it exactly.'

'You don't want to play on the team, and you don't want me to go into the ring?'

Jack grinned delightedly. 'Maybe it would be better not. That way might lead to discovery.'

'And what am I to do while you get yourself over the border?'

'You go to my restaurant and sit about in the background. I'll give you a note to the manager. If you look kind of indignantified, you'll find no one will come intruding on your privacy.'

There was a long silence. The baseball player said at last: 'I've got a wife and kids. I don't want no prison sentence.'

'Why should you get one?'

'That's right, why should I?'

'Besides which, the little honorarium I had in mind is sort of calculated to relieve your mental distressfulness.'

The baseball player shook his head. 'Brother, I don't do this for dough. I do this to help another Negro out of a jam.'

And the plan worked. A couple of days later Jack, having slid out of town on the pretence of going to Cedar Lake for a week's fishing trip, was one of a group of light-hearted Negro Giants bringing a cargo of baseball trophies over the Canadian border.

Lucille hadn't had any difficulty in getting out of the country with most of their possessions. Husband and wife met as planned in Hamilton, Ontario. The world lay open to them: *all the world except home.* For the next seven years Jack was to travel in Europe, in South and Central America. He was to defeat Frank Moran and the Russian catch-as-catch-can wrestler Spoul. He was to visit Russia and to lead a hectic and unsatisfactory life in show business in London. He was to lose his title in Cuba, and act as a spy and as a bull-fighter in Spain; he was to come home at last, too late to see the mother for whose sake he had gone into exile.

With Lucille and his nephew Gus Rhodes beside him he boarded the liner *Corinthian* at Montreal on 29 June 1913. A hundred white passengers heard that he was to sail on their liner without enthusiasm. When the identity was disclosed of the big Negro who came on board with two cars and eighteen trunks they held indignation meetings on the wharf and were only pacified by the assurance that Johnson's party were to be given their meals in their staterooms and not permitted to mingle with the plaster saints on the passenger list.

Elwood Godman, Assistant United States District Attorney, probably summed up the American official attitude to Johnson's escape while on bail: 'This may solve the whole affair,' he said. 'The passengers may mutiny and heave him away on an iceberg.'

It was left to Gus Rhodes to sum up the future, as the *Corinthian* sailed.

'We're the Three Musketeers,' he said. Maybe Jack understood the literary allusion: maybe not. The benefits of education by the cinema had yet to be widely diffused.

'I'll tell you what we are,' he said at last, 'we're three fugitives from home and fortune. What we'll find over in England in the way of a living is anybody's guess.'

Gus scoffed and Lucille protested. The champion of the world was somebody anyone in the world would want to pay money to see. But Jack remained unconvinced. He was certain that his record would count against him in England at least. There would be a welcome only from the curious.

As things turned out, he was right indeed. When he appeared in England in 1913, there stood against him a sentence of one year and a fine of $200 for his conviction under the Mann Act. In many places his sparring act was roundly booed, though counter-cheers were generally not slow to sound. At the old South London Music Hall he had a mixed reception. At the Euston Theatre of Varieties there was a demonstration against even the women who appeared in the same programme as he did. It was suggested by his critics that his appearance on the bill was on all fours with that of the man tried for the Camden Town murder—in other words, sheer, vile notoriety had its market value. The Reverend F. B. Meyer protested against his engagement as a music hall 'star', and the Variety Artists Federation were also anxious to see the back of him. When he went to Wolverhampton, the President of the Free Church protested; his boxing exhibition was cancelled in one town. The Swansea Watch Committee demanded that he shouldn't sully the fair name of their city. When he slipped over to Paris to fight Moran, he got into trouble for hitting an American in the street, his excuse being that he supposed the fellow had insulted Lucille.

A few months later there was a warrant out for his arrest in London for failing to answer a summons for using obscene language in Coventry Street. Then—after his defeat by Willard—in the autumn of 1915 there was a disgusting fracas at the Hippodrome, Preston, where Johnson's revue, *Seconds Out*, was being performed to a tepidly interested audience. Jack du Maurier, Johnson's manager and a performer in the show, had found his boss agreeable and charming while business was good. Now, however, when faced with failure, the other side of Johnson's nature was revealed. When Johnson sent for him and dismissed him, du Maurier produced the bill for his salary and his fare to London. Instantly Johnson became vicious, hitting out as if in the ring and injuring the structure of his unfortunate victim's eye. For a boxer to resort to his fists against a non-boxer is a transgression against the unwritten law of the craft, as well as against the Statute Book of the land. Johnson's barbarity on this occasion cost him the admiration of not a few who felt he had been persecuted for his colour and his failure to curb his natural instincts. It also cost him £1,075: for which sum there was (in the defendant's absence) a verdict for the plaintiff.

Such was the future the Three Musketeers were sailing to as their ship left Montreal Harbour in the summer of 1913. It cannot have been a rewarding experience for Lucille who had suffered so much before being permitted to link her fortune with Johnson's. But there were times that were less sordid and shining hours amid the encircling gloom.

There were, for example (if Johnson's own version of them can be trusted) the visit to Russia after the Moran fight in 1914, and the work of espionage in Madrid after America had joined the Allies.

The trip to Russia was a curious expedition, for it was undertaken partly as a sightseeing visit and partly as a barnstorming tour by the world's champion. After all these years we have only Johnson's word for what happened to him, but if his account is to be trusted, it appears that the visit was melodramatic in the highest degree. One of its highlights was the occasion when Johnson was attacked by a drunk in St Petersburg, an incident with which one might have thought the conqueror of Jeffries would be well qualified to cope single-handed. But not at all. Before Johnson could extricate himself from the struggle, twelve soldiers rushed to the rescue—of the drunk. Johnson set about them gleefully, despite the fact that one at least drew his bayonet, and had knocked three of them out by the time the police arrived to restore order.

But Jack, even by his own account, never had much success with the army while in Russia. After his exhibitions had been cancelled, due to the closing of the theatres on the eve of war, it was to an army barracks that he was summoned to be given his marching orders.

What was his offence?

It appeared that he was a friend of the Negro, George Thomas. He did not deny this? It was true? Very well, then, no doubt he would work out the consequences of this friendship for himself.

But, for Jack, it wasn't as easy as that. When he had arrived in Russia, George Thomas was the first friend to greet him. He was a remarkable man; a Negro who had made a fortune as a business man in St Petersburg and could boast the entrée to the Court and the friendship of the Czar of All the Russias.

'I want you to meet everyone of importance over here, Jack,' he had said, and had taken him to every party given by the Grand Dukes during his stay in St Petersburg. Then, as his stay neared its end, he had told him in a conspiratorial whisper that he had someone more important than a Grand Duke for him to meet that night.

'The Czar, no doubt?'

George Thomas laughed. 'Oh no, not the Czar. Someone more important than the Czar.'

But it hadn't appeared that there was anyone specially important at the party that night. George Thomas himself spent most of his time talking to a bearded monk as big as Jim Jeffries, who smelt strongly, and ate and drank voraciously. 'Never forget him, Jack,' George Thomas had said at the end of the evening. 'His name is Rasputin, and he is a Man of Destiny.'

It was of Rasputin that Jack was thinking as the General ordered him out of the barracks, and out of Russia. The *troika* took him at once to George's house: if they followed him, it couldn't be helped—what more could they do than exile him?

George greeted him with a smile. 'So they've turned you out?'

It suddenly occurred to Jack that George had always known his friendship would be fatal in the end.

'You knew they would!'

George shrugged his shoulders. He didn't look broken-hearted.

'Listen, George—you're a Negro. There's a bond between us, the closest bond among the living. Why am I ordered out of Russia? Is it because of you? Is it because of your friend Rasputin?'

George didn't answer. He went to his desk and unlocked a drawer. From it he took a key. 'Wait here, Jack, I shan't be a minute.'

When he returned he had a packet of papers, corded and sealed, in his hands. 'I want you to take these for me to London. One day I'll let you know what you must do with them. Until then I can only tell you what you *mustn't* do. You mustn't let them fall into the hands of the Germans. Not if it costs you your life.' His voice sank. 'What are they? I'll tell you. They're copies of the private notes passed between the Kaiser and the Czar.'

He stared at Jack as if he could not bear to let him go. 'You mustn't let them get them. Not if they shoot you against a wall for it,' he said in a whisper.

He left George Thomas's house with the packet in his pocket. He knew that one day—and one day soon—that packet was destined to play an important part in his life. But where and how remained a mystery.

As for George Thomas, he was to remain in Russia, rich and respected, even when those who basked in the shadow of his patronage were swept away. Not even the Revolution was to get rid of George. He side-stepped it as neatly as Johnson side-stepped the challenge from Langford. The next time Jack heard from him he was sitting pretty in Constantinople, a mystery man still and as rich as ever.

As for Jack, he made his way through Eastern Europe to England. It was no easy journey. Most of his possessions were lost when a luggage van disappeared in Warsaw, but the packet of papers had never left his pocket. The last lap of the trip was particularly exciting. The train for the French frontier left Berlin with scores of desperate people clinging to the footboards and buffers. At Boulogne there were hundreds hanging about the quayside in hope of bribing someone to give them passage to England. One man offered Jack £500 if he would smuggle him in. 'A spy for a certainty,' he said to Lucille and turned to assure the Customs Officer that he had nothing to declare. Surely a packet of letters, even if sealed with the Czar's private seal, wasn't dutiable?

X

✦✦

AUSTRALIA HAD BEEN DAZED and bewildered by the news that Jack had won the world's heavyweight championship from Tommy Burns. America couldn't believe when Jack beat Jeffries that it meant what it seemed to mean; that a Negro was the greatest fighter in the world at any weight. America didn't want to believe it, and White Americans regarded it as a duty, at once patriotic and religious, to find themselves a Caucasian good enough not only to beat but utterly to humiliate the man who had taunted and spurned both Burns and Jeffries.

The search for a White Hope was about as otherworldly an enterprise as the search for the Holy Grail, and about as likely to command success. The palpable fact was that not one of the White Hopes bringing to birth the gigantic headlines from Maine to the Coast could have lived with Johnson for three rounds, if Johnson were in the mood to cut proceedings short. Tommy Burns was probably still the best white fighter in the world, and Burns came after an era of supermen: the great Corbett, first of the scientific boxers; the lanky, freckled freak, Bob Fitzsimmons, bald and spindle-shanked but with a teak barrel of a torso; and the gigantic Jim Jeffries with a left jab like a jolt from a piston. The younger generation weren't fit to lace these heroes' shoes; and these heroes already belonged to history.

There were, it is true, boxers in Jack Johnson's class at this stage in the game, but they were all Negroes. There were, in particular three pastmasters. Sam McVey and Sam Langford (the Big Smoke and the Little Smoke); and Joe Jeannette, the Master Strategist, of New Jersey.

Of the three, Jeannette was the one least compelling to the public imagination of his time, yet he was good enough to have been champion of the world almost any day in the immediate post-World-War-I history of the ring. He fought Johnson eight times and no contest between these two looked like less than the climax of a blood feud. Once, and once only, Jeannette won a decision—that was on a foul in two rounds in 1905. Johnson twice won on points, once over fifteen rounds and once over three, though this last battle is sometimes described as a draw or a no-decision bout in the record books. One of the remaining bouts ended in a draw; in the others no verdict was given.

It was particularly noticeable that Johnson was never prepared to risk his title against Jeannette (nor, of course, against Langford or McVey) after he had won the heavyweight championship. The two men were bitter foes, and there would have been no question of having a comfortable ride to a points decision with Joe on the losing end of the bout. At that, after he had retired Johnson was prepared to admit that Jeannette, when little more than a novice, had given him one of the closest-run battles of his life. But in fact in one particular Jeannette was made for Johnson. Joe liked to carry the battle to his man; and the champion was never happier than when tackling a forcing fighter.

Jeannette was a black Adonis; a magnificently proportioned man, a couple of inches under six feet in height, with a strong torso, splendidly developed legs and handsome features. He was never a braggart nor a clown, but led a quiet, disciplined life. After his retirement he became celebrated in New Jersey as a teacher of boxing: it was in his gymnasium at Hoboken that Jim Braddock was discovered by Joe Gould.

Jeannette was in his twenty-fourth year when he first boxed as a professional because a friend dared him to see how he would get on in the ring. In his second year he four times fought Johnson, lost to Sam Langford, and won other important contests, including one against Black Bill. It was a good beginning—far too good, as it happened. He had established himself already as one of the hardest men in the game to beat, and the leading white boxers already drew the colour line against him. This drove one of the few Negro boxers of the period against whom no breath of scandal was ever uttered, to seek his living outside his own country, and he naturally sought sanctuary in Paris where Hugh D. McIntosh was drawing full houses to watch Negroes who couldn't persuade Johnson into the ring beat the hide off all other contenders.

It was in Paris that Jeannette fought the most famous battle of his life. This was his return contest with Sam McVey on 17 April 1909, when McVey was only twenty-three and Jeannette twenty-eight. The two men had already fought a twenty-round contest which had bored the spectators so completely that few of them remained in their seats when the referee raised McVey's hand at the end of it. But the return match was quite a different affair. It was the most tremendous battle that ever took place in the history of boxing since prize ring days. Disgusted by the insipid bout between the two men three months earlier, only 2,000 spectators (largely Americans at that) turned up to see whether Jeannette was good enough to turn the tables on his chief rival, even if it were not in a match for the world's championship.

This time there was no doubt about the seriousness of the occasion. Jeannette and McVey didn't like the rumours that the previous fight had been a mere sparring match; and they didn't like each other either. They agreed now to fight to a finish; and nothing —not the police, nor the Red Cross, nor the Fire Brigade—could get them to agree to any other arrangement to settle the dispute as to which was the better man.

The fight began in McVey's favour. As soon as the first bell went he sprang from his corner, flung over a thunderclap of a right swing that set Jeannette rocking on his heels, and followed it with the sort of left jab which has finished not merely many good bouts, but also many good careers. Jeannette keeled over instantly, and hats flew up at the ringside from those who had backed the favourite and were convinced that they had seen him win in the first round.

But as it happened the fight was to last a little longer than that. Joe Jeannette hauled himself off the floor to beat the count, and fell into a clinch against the ropes. McVey shrugged him off and pumped long lefts and rights into him, but Jeannette rode the punches, and, though giving slightly at the knees, somehow weathered the storm. The first round, however, was only an earnest of things to come. McVey was the dominant; McVey was the Emperor Jones; McVey was the executioner. The only thing was that McVey, although he had Jeannette's head on the block, couldn't quite strike it off his neck. He blunted both fists, as he must have blunted an axe, or landed with the sound of a warhead striking home against the mark.

Jeannette stumbled round the ring under this murderous assault and was regularly swept off his feet to hit the floor like a sack of cement dropped from a roof. Somehow, however, he was always able to scramble up before the count was finished. By the time the nineteenth round was over he had been stretched across the floor of the ring twenty-one times. You could count the twenty-one little red puddles. Moreover he had yet to knock McVey off his feet— indeed he wasn't to do so until the fight reached the thirty-ninth round.

But that didn't mean Joe Jeannette was a mere punchbag. Though it couldn't be said he was giving as good as he got, he was far from being exclusively on the receiving end of the barrage. You see, Jeannette was fighting to a plan, a plan worked out by his wily second, Willie Lewis, who was later to handle Moran against Johnson. Lewis's point was that McVey's head was a block of granite against which some of the best men in the business had splintered their fists without making the Negro blink. He urged Jeannette not to aim a blow at McVey's skull until he had worn Sam down by a ruthless and ceaseless battery to the body. True, McVey's body (Johnson left it on record in an unsolicited testimony) was like teak, but teak makes a better target than granite. For ten rounds—for fifteen—for twenty—Joe Jeannette crunched his fists into McVey's ribs and belly and over his heart; and McVey stayed on his feet and swept Jeannette up into the air with uppercuts and power-driven right swings.

The worst moment for Joe came in the sixteenth round when Sam slipped a lead and hit him with a right hook that seemed to twist his head right round on his neck. Only the bell saved Jeannette that time; and for the next couple of rounds he knew as much about what he was doing as a man in a hypnotic trance. At the end of the seventeenth round he didn't know where he was, and couldn't find his own corner; and when Willie Lewis at last dragged him to his stool he had to empty the water bucket over his head to revive him, while kicking aside the police who attempted to throw him out of the building for assisting at a probable case of manslaughter. Only the bell for the eighteenth round saved the situation. Jeannette seemed quite ready to battle on, and the police found that they would have to face a second French Revolution from the holders of ringside seats if they attempted to stop the fight.

By the time the bell went for the end of the round there was a doctor with an oxygen bag waiting for Jeannette in his corner. He remained there for the rest of the fight pumping just enough life into the half-dead man in the minute intervals to return him to the ring for further butcheries to be wreaked upon him.

The oxygen revived the Master Strategist, though what would be the reaction of the referee to the use of such a stimulant in the ring to-day defies the imagination of one who feels competent to prophesy the *obiter dicta* of sergeant-majors in any given circumstances. From the twentieth round onwards Jeannette's counter-attacks began to take effect. McVey started to back-pedal, slinging punches from every angle as he went. Now and again the punches found their mark, and it was always Jeannette who hit the canvas. But a knock-down blow seemed to have no effect on him; he came up cool as ever and went in with head down and hands flailing away to the short ribs.

The tide really turned after the thirty-first round, though it was not until eight rounds later that Jeannette lifted McVey off his feet for the first time. A left to the point that would have gravelled a gorilla made a hinge in McVey's straight back, and he sank slowly to the ground. Once again it looked all over, and the crowd was on its feet shouting with the uninhibited bliss of cannibals at the boiling of a missionary. But even this wasn't the end—it was barely the beginning of the end. McVey tottered to his feet, his eyes glazing. Then as Jeannette leaped at him, he sprang forward and shook him from head to foot with a straight left that set his head rocking on his shoulders. Till the end of the round the two Negroes stood toe to toe slashing at each other with rolling swings and prodigious uppercuts. Their bronze bodies gleamed under a thick coating of scarlet. Neither attempted defence. This battle was not to be won by evading punishment: it was won by remaining upright when the other man was bludgeoned into insensibility or death.

From the thirty-ninth round, when McVey first sprawled across the canvas to the end of the fight, Sam was to be knocked off his feet nineteen times; Jeannette, from first to last, went down twenty-seven times. In the last ten rounds McVey went through the motions of combat with the helpless ferocity of a blind black panther at bay. His right eye was closed completely: his second had to slit open his left so that he could get an occasional glimpse of his opponent in the intervals between the gushing of blood from his all but severed eyebrow. The bone in his nose was cracked in two places. When he spat across the ring, a red stream spurted from his chopped lips. This was the man who had so nearly won on a knock-out with the first two blows of the fight!

The contest had begun at eleven o'clock on a cool spring evening. It did not end till three in the morning, by which time every night bird in Paris was hanging around the doors shouting the news of the latest knock-down to be echoed across the empty streets, picked up and repeated by the singers in the cabarets of the Left Bank. McVey was lying on the floor vomiting blood! Jeannette was draped across the ropes, spewing his guts out! The two of them were lying together, end to end, and the police were arresting everyone from Theodore Vienne to Dan McKettrick, Jeannette's manager, as accomplices in a double manslaughter. . . . So the rumours spread, and meanwhile history went on in the making.

It was all Jeannette now. He was stalking his man like a big black cat: shooting his blows in under arms that flapped helplessly. Almost at will he landed hooks and jabs on that granite head upon which Willie Lewis had warned him so many great fighters had broken their hands. McVey staggered round the ring, incapable of locating his opponent—in the forty-ninth round he hit out completely at random, for he was blindfolded with swollen flesh and a mask of blood. When the bell went for the next round, he didn't move. He couldn't get up. He could fight no more. Jeannette had beaten him.

So ended the most ferocious battle and the sternest test of endurance ever known under Queensberry Rules. The contest staggered the sporting world: it would not have believed that there were any two men on earth who could show such powers of fortitude and sustained fury. There were those who demanded that the winner should be given his chance with Johnson, but Jeannette had no illusions on that score. He knew full well that he had shown form altogether too impressive to be welcomed as a rival by the champion. He fought other fights in Paris, beating Sandy Ferguson on points before returning to America via London. In the States he got several contests with Langford (beating him on points in 1915, but generally losing to him) though he challenged for a title bout in vain.

In 1914 he returned to Paris to fight Carpentier at Lunar Park. It was a great event and drew 6,000 spectators who must have considered they got their money's worth. Carpentier forced the pace from the start, and coming out of a clinch, dropped Jeannette with a one-two in the first round. Carpentier and the crowd considered the battle as good as won, but those who remembered what had happened to McVey, knew that sending Jeannette down for a long count in the first round was by no means an augury of victory. The bout was close and interesting. Carpentier's speed and scientific skill were pitted in vain against Jeannette's classic defence and unsappable courage. Over the second half of the contest the Negro came into his own. More than once his clever defence had made Carpentier look like a fool; once, indeed, when the white man slipped, Jeannette won applause by solicitously helping him to his feet—he might have been his father. In the twelfth round Jeannette was magnificent and Carpentier was swept before his assault like a leaf in a high wind.

At the end of the fourteenth round Jeannette was in the lead. The two men went to their corners to puff almost audibly against the sea-deep silence of the Vel d'Hiver. Women clenched their handkerchiefs in scented palms: bosoms swelled and fell more than bosoms normally swell and fall even in Paris. Descamps worked like a maniac on the battered frame of the Orchid Man. The bell went for the last round.

The clenched handkerchiefs were squeezed tighter than ever. Would he come up, would he face the final music—the glorious Georges Carpentier? Or would he wilt, on the stool in his corner, fading and failing until the towel fluttered in, as against Young Snowball and Billy Papke? And as the bell rang, the ghost of Carpentier rose like Jehovah in his wrath and hurled itself like Jehovah's thunderbolt across the ring at the inscrutable ebony statue that was Jeannette. The tattered hero carried the battle to the master, like some broken figure from the south storming the barricades of privilege and establishment. The right uppercut sang, strident as the music of the spheres; Jeannette's legs shrank, Jeannette's body tottered. Jeannette went rockily round the ropes.

The splendid straight left rocked his head back. The right over the heart doubled him up like a poisoned creature. Carpentier stood off and hooked the black granite jaw with jabs whose rattling power could almost be felt in their hurtful fury by the stiff-shirted *virtuosi* in the front row of the stalls. Orchids trembled, bosoms heaved. The white man sprang in like a snow-leopard, snarled as he shot in fang-sharp blows, leaped clear of the sluggish counter artillery. Jeannette rolled round the ring helpless and hopeless.

The bell rang against the tumult: the referee pulled the men apart. The hand he held up was Jeannette's. Carpentier was beaten—the last stand was in vain, romance had *not* come up with the nine-fifteen. . . .

Perhaps that was Jeannette's final flicker, the last little flash in the pan. Perhaps he was lucky to get the verdict: certainly nearly all the papers who discussed the decision considered that he could consider himself a fortunate man to have weathered the storm and even more fortunate to have received the decision.

But victory did him no good. There was, you see, only one bit of good—only one good turn you *could* do him. You could decide, on the strength of his victory over Carpentier, the top man in Europe, that he was eligible for a contest with Jack Johnson for the world's title. After all, Jack was at hand. He was in Europe, too, and prepared to defend his title—three months after Jeannette beat Carpentier—in a bout with Moran in Paris. But Jeannette, there on the spot and an ace with the box-office, Jack Johnson chose to by-pass, as he had by-passed him ever since the day he had won the title. Jeannette smiled philosophically, and admitted that he was not much surprised. He was rising thirty-five now, three years older than Johnson; and he pinned his hopes to the belief that Jack might consider him past his best. Perhaps Jack did: but he also knew that he was much past his own best too. He was taking no risks against a man whose form he knew and respected all too well.

But if he gave Jeannette a wide berth he had taken a chance, in the final month of 1913, with the Negro, Jim Johnson, whom he boxed over ten rounds in Paris's Premierland. Jim Johnson was a superb fighter, though Jack professed to regard his contest with him as nothing more than a work-out to prepare him for the bout with Moran. Yet the fight was almost fatal to him. Jack boxed feebly and was knocked around the ring during the final rounds, so that he was certainly saved from a knock-out when the bell sounded for the end of the tenth round. The referee's verdict of a draw was received with undisguised contempt by the Paris crowd—they booed Jack as he sat in his corner protesting vigorously that he had broken his arm in the third round and had only gone on suffering virtual crucifixion as a mark of respect for his beloved public. The beloved public even booed the doctor who examined Jack in the ring and testified to his broken arm; their view seemed to be that a broken arm was neither here nor there. They would settle for a broken neck.

XI

✦✦

JACK JOHNSON MAY HAVE MISCALCULATED when he agreed to fight his namesake Jim. He may have been unnecessarily prudent when he expressed reluctance to meet Jeannette, whose superior he could claim to be, such a consideration as fitness for a title bout being (somewhat handsomely) taken for granted. But the article in Jack's faith that chiefly fascinated the public had nothing to do with either of these claimants—it was concerned with his grading of the two main contenders for a bout for the title. These two were, of course, Sam McVey and Sam Langford: Sam and Sambo—the Big Smoke and the Little Smoke.

There is a pleasant story that the two men met for the first time in a boxing promoter's office, when McVey drew from his pocket a silver-mounted pipe which he handed reverently to Langford. 'My dad gave me this,' he is reported to have said, 'and he told me, "Keep it, Sam, until you meet an uglier nigger than yourself." I reckon that pipe, Mr Langford, has been won by you.' As the verdict of a judge of beauty competitions, McVey's rating was probably correct; but the point that has gripped the imagination of the boxing world is not so much whether Langford was even less of an Adonis than McVey, but whether he was even more of an indestructible fighter. Their contemporaries believed that Jack Johnson in his heart of hearts considered Langford the more dangerous rival, which was why (while regularly refusing to meet him again after their first encounter on 26 April 1906) he professed a critical disregard of this rival and a theatrical awe of McVey, whom he was always tolerably sure of beating.

Now these base suspicions over-simplify the problem. Johnson's critics always push their case too far. They readily proclaim that Jack was lucky to win his one fight with Langford—that the Little Smoke knocked him off his feet—that Johnson would always sneak out of a tavern if he saw Langford through the smoke-haze at the other end of the bar. Well, it is true that Jack had no intention whatever of meeting Langford a second time: but that is about all that is true in the general statement of the case against him. It is certainly not true that he barred Langford because he knew from experience that Langford would beat him if they met again. Experience suggested quite the opposite; on the occasion of their single battle Jack had won one of the consummate victories of his career.

Sam Langford, 'The Boston Tar Baby,' was eight years younger than his great rival. The most remarkable thing about him was his size, especially when it is remembered that in his day he was considered the most annihilating puncher in the business. Sam was 5 feet 7½ inches tall, and weighed, when he fought Johnson, 11 stone 2 pounds. At his best and at his heaviest he was never more than a very light middleweight indeed.

Physically he was a freak. He was a short man who had got hold of a very tall man's arms and a giant's torso. His reach was seventy-three inches; his chest (expanded) was forty-seven inches. He was tough, not like McVey, as if hewn out of teak: he was tough and indestructible as if compounded of india-rubber.

Like Jack himself, he left home young, to seek a fortune that somehow always eluded him. He was fifteen when he first arrived in Boston from Nova Scotia. He had ridden the rods all the way, eaten crusts and drunk water. He was thin and tired, but as always bubbling with good humour. Moreover he had a friend—a yellow dog who stuck to his heels as if it were his shadow. Joe Woodman, who staged fights at the Lenox Athletic Club, gave Langford his first chance, after feeding him and his dog and allowing them to sleep on the club-house floor in return for sweeping out his drugstore. He also staked Sam to an entry fee in an amateur tournament, in which the boxer won a gold watch—a useful embellishment to a man who hadn't got a waistcoat to put it in.

No matter, Langford's career was founded! Woodman allowed him to appear at the bottom of the bill at the Club, and he always won. In 1903, his second season, he fought thirty times, and though once beaten, outpointed Joe Gans, in an overweight match not involving the 'Old Master's' lightweight title. In the following year Langford fought Joe Walcott, and was given a draw after fifteen ferocious rounds. The decision was held in contempt by every spectator present who did not happen to have put his money on Walcott.

Even though he was probably robbed of the world's welter-weight championship, Langford earned a matchless reputation from this fight. He was admitted by the experts to be the most promising battler seen for years, and a great prospect for a title in due course. But there was plenty of opposition. There were such Negro boxers as Dave Holly of Philadelphia who, aided by a defence an income-tax inspector couldn't have penetrated, beat Sam more often than Sam beat him. There was Young Peter Jackson, as hard a nut to crack as most; and there was Larry Temple, who beat Langford the first time they met.

The victories these men notched against Sam were genuinely scored to their credit, for the Boston Tar Baby at this time was desperately fighting for his right to a place in the sun. But not all the defeats on Sam's record—and there are few enough among his 250 fights—came about because Sam was the worse man. Not a few were matters of arrangement. Langford and McVey fought each other fifteen times. Sometimes they fought in earnest and knocked each other out. Sometimes they merely went through the motions; and now and again, when the act had an over-rehearsed look about it, the crowd booed enthusiastically—it was apt to be the only enthusiasm shown on such occasions. The ten-round no-decision bout in New York on 30 November 1915, for example, was less of a fight than a love feast. The spectators said it looked more like a Christmas family reunion than a battle. Two more ten-rounders early in 1916 were described as New Year Parties with a good deal of back-slapping thrown in.

But it mustn't be supposed that Big Sam and Sambo never set about each other in earnest. Up to 1915 the bouts between the two were generally spontaneous and fierce. In 1911, for example, the pair fought a draw in Paris, which even those connoisseurs of the blood lust who had sated themselves on the classic Jeannette-McVey contest admitted was entirely adequate. The fights in Australia were generally regarded as really impressive, especially the last bout in 1911, when McVey won over twenty rounds. Again there was the series contested between the two men in Australia in 1912, including several marvellous victories by Langford. Real stuff—and red-hot stuff at that! These engagements stand to the credit of both men. McVey and Langford didn't *always* treat each other as routine, run-of-the-mill engagements. For the record, Langford beat McVey four times, suffering two defeats.

Langford paid two trips to England. On the first occasion he travelled over to fight Tiger Smith at the National Sporting Club in 1907, his chief reason being that he could no longer find contests in America with men of his own class and weight. His departure was a dramatic affair. He arrived a few minutes before S.S. *Ivernia* was due to sail and behind him came a flock of camp-followers all of whom were under the impression that they had been invited to England too. It was with the greatest difficulty that Sam was lured away from his supporters and locked into a cabin, while the rest of the gang gathered round the bewildered journalist who had arranged the fight for Sam and was believed by all present to have their return tickets in his waistcoat pocket. At last the hoot of the steamer drowned the clamour of the mob, and as the *Ivernia* passed down New York Harbour Langford's face appeared at a porthole. The camp followers ceased their catcalls and turned reverently towards their master. It was always possible he had a message for them. As a matter of fact, he had. Through the porthole Langford blew a tremendous raspberry at all present. Then his head disappeared from view.

The fight with Tiger Smith had its serio-comic background too, according to Sam Austin, the New York journalist who arranged the bout after Langford had parted brass tacks with his old friend and manager, Joe Woodman. Smith was the bigger man, and a warm favourite with the British fight fans. Langford began slowly, with a view to getting the odds against himself lengthened. At the end of the third round the odds against the Negro were as long as could be expected, and Sam came out to commit execution with a confident look on his face. He hit Tiger Smith with a left hook that split his eyebrow wide open, lifted him into the air and dropped him, out to the world, in his own corner.

Sam had done the job, but once again had done it too well. Just as it was impossible for him to get himself contests with white boxers in America, so now, by his decisive victory over Smith he had scared the English challengers out of sight. There was nothing left to do but return to the States, make friends with Joe Woodman again and get himself signed up for routine engagements with Larry Temple (somewhere near his own weight) and such heavies as Jim Barry and Young Peter Jackson.

Once in a very long while he was able to persuade a white man to share a ring with him. One such was Jim Flynn, the Pueblo fire-man, who had lasted eleven rounds with Jack Johnson; another was Sandy Ferguson, a giant from Boston. Sam did not pull his punches with either, and on comparative form looked a heavier puncher than Johnson.

But Jack had the world on his side. He was the established challenger. No one was going to stand in his way till he got Tommy Burns into a ring with the world's championship at stake. The

English public, disgusted by Johnson's treatment of the National Sporting Club, hardened its heart against him, and decided to rub along with Langford instead. Sam was invited over again to fight Iron Hague of Mexborough, the British champion, at the National Sporting Club, in 1909. Sam was broke, and anxious for any work on any terms. For once he got very good terms indeed—a payment of £2,500, the highest reward he ever received for a contest.

Hague was a big hunk of a man, slow, but next door to indestructible. He loathed training: it was always said of him (somewhat over-enthusiastically) that he might beat any champion in the world except John Barleycorn—whereupon Hague, no scholar, would clench his fist, exhibit his biceps, and challenge this fellow Barleycorn to come on.

The Langford party was not frightened of Hague; and a few minutes before the fight (according to American folk-lore) Joe Woodman wormed his way into a betting club where he backed Sam for ten thousand at even money. Only when he got back to the ring-side and told the boxer what he had done did the enormity of his offence dawn on him: he had the cheque for £2,500 in his pocket and had mentally banked it as ten thousand, its equivalent in dollars in that faraway day and age. As soon as Sam pointed out the discrepancy in the rate of exchange, Joe Woodman fell in a faint in the corner of the ring. Sam, fortunately, kept his senses; though he was almost worried out of his wits by his fears of offending against the National Sporting Club's code of rules, with which he was unfamiliar. As it happened the result was determined by one rule which he knew tolerably well. When he spreadeagled Hague with that famous right hook and the count went to ten, the fight was his. The news was enough to bring Joe Woodman out of his coma.

Even so, the fight had had its frightening moments, quite apart from its financial aspects. In the second round Hague landed a mighty punch on Langford's jaw and toppled him on the floor. When the contest was over, the Negro told referee Eugene Corri that this was the heaviest punch he had ever received in his life.

Sam enjoyed his trip to England, even if he did shock some of the Corinthians by his brash ways; as for instance when he told the National Sporting Club that he always carried his own referee—resolving their perplexity by holding up his clenched right fist in explanation. But England brought him no nearer to the dream of his life: a return contest with Johnson. And—short of Johnson—there really did not seem to be anyone in the world worth fighting.

If there *was* anyone, it was Stanley Ketchel; like Langford, also a middleweight. One would have thought that a Langford-Ketchel fight (or possibly a Ketchel-Langford fight) would have been just the bout the world was waiting to see. After all, the men were designed by nature to be rivals, whereas Hague was thirty-eight pounds heavier than Langford and Johnson only a pound or two less than Hague. But Ketchel was reluctant to put it to the test, to win or lose it all. He was, notoriously, as game as a pebble, but his manager persuaded him that it was bad business to let the world find out which was the supreme man at the weight in a full scale long-distance contest. In the end, the two met for the only time in a six-round no-decision contest in Philadelphia a year after Langford had battered Hague to submission in London.

What should have been the fight of the century was a desperate disappointment. The two men gave a sedate exhibition of the airs and graces of their trade, neither so far demeaning himself as to launch a punch in anger at his opponent (or partner). It may be that Langford in particular felt himself dedicated to a piece of pious deception. There was always the hope that, if he didn't look too good, Ketchel would one day consent to meet him in a real bout with the championship at stake.

But there was to be no middleweight title fight for Sam Langford. Whether or not his genteel deportment had gulled Ketchel into assuming that he wasn't really so very formidable after all, there was never any chance for Sam to test the champion in a full scale contest, for a few months later Ketchel was murdered by a ranch hand in Conway, Missouri, who suspected him of paying attentions to his girl friend.

Sam Langford had to content himself with the assurance that he was the greatest middleweight fighting in the heavyweight division —indeed, he was arguably the greatest middleweight since Sayers. But he never got a second chance against Jack Johnson. There remains on his record only that points decision given to Jack in April 1906, after fifteen very exciting rounds. That battle, when Sam was hardly out of his novitiate and Jack was not yet at his peak, took place three weeks after Langford had fought fifteen rounds with Jeannette. Years afterwards Langford admitted that Johnson had given him 'the only real beating' he ever had, but pointed out that at the time he was twenty-nine pounds lighter than his conqueror. Langford was twice sent down for long counts—the first in the eighth round would have given Johnson a knock-out victory if the referee hadn't been generous to the man on the floor in tolling off the seconds. As it was, Langford was put on a stretcher and hustled to hospital at the end of the bout.

After this Johnson barred Langford in the ring, in the street, and as has been said, even in the tavern. Once they met in a Boston bar, and Sam challenged Jack there and then to a turn-up in the cellars for the $1,000 he always kept in his pocket in the hope of such a chance presenting itself. Jack smiled gleamingly and waved apologetic hands. He was, it appeared, wearing a new suit and didn't want to get it creased. Some other time, perhaps. . . . And Jack retreated, while Langford, his face a study in frustration, kept his place at the bar, hopelessly buying drinks for those friends who had witnessed Jack's humiliation with the $1,000 note that was never going to be worth saving for a better purpose.

At the end of his career in the ring—*at* the end of it, not after its end—Langford went blind. His final fight, at the age of thirty-seven, was against an old rival, Jim Flynn, in Mexico City. Sam was as near blind as made no difference, but boxed by ear and knocked his man out in three rounds. The old battering around the optic nerves had done their worst after those two hundred and fifty contests. An operation failed to save Sam's sight.

He retired, penniless, to Harlem, and Mayor La Guardia found a job for him in 1937, as watchman in a New York armoury housing the 115th Regiment. So poor Sam's end was in his beginning. As he had swept out Joe Woodman's drugstore over twenty years before, so now he took his broom and went to work over the armoury floors: only, this time, there was no friendly yellow dog to keep him company; nothing but his memories—and never a call from a friend for a man who once had been the heaviest puncher in the world.

Not, of course, that Jack Johnson would admit that Sam Langford was any such thing. He was patronizing to Langford to the very end of his career, and after. He declared that you could tangle poor little Sambo up in knots and pen him in a corner where he hadn't a chance to unleash that murderous right hand of his.

Now was Jack being honest when he lightly wrote off Langford as a serious opponent? It should be remembered, perhaps, in Johnson's defence that he maintained his opinion long after he went into retirement, when a generous tribute to Sam would no longer have cost him anything. Indeed, it would have been quite in character for Jack to indulge in a satisfying sneer at his critics by admitting, once he was safely out of the game, that he had recognized Langford's ability all the time, but had fooled them all by keeping him at bay. Yet he did nothing of the sort: he simply stuck to it that there was neither fame nor fortune to be gained from beating Langford a second time. He may have been right about the fame; he was surely wrong about the fortune.

'Here you are, Jack . . . just sign there, on the line. Ten thousand dollars, and half of it in advance, for fighting Sam Langford.'

'No, thank you, mistah. Ask someone else. I just plain ain't interested.'

And then there would come the letters from 'Peggy' Bettinson in London, reminding Jack of his pledge to fight Sam at the National Sporting Club.

'Jack,' pleaded George Considine, one of those who had raised the $5,000 to send Fitzpatrick and Johnson to London on the track of Tommy Burns, 'you never did a stupider thing than when you threw over Fitzpatrick. It's cost you pretty well every friend you have in America. You've *got* to honour the plans Fitzpatrick made for you.'

'Listen, Mr Considine—I've *got* to do nothing. I'm the best man in the world and I don't have to take orders from anyone. See this letter from Mr Bettinson? Into the fire it goes! That's what I think of Sam Fitzpatrick and the plans he forced me into.'

Langford! Langford! Always Langford. . . . Why didn't they take some notice of Sam McVey, the proper size for a man like Johnson to be stacked up against? The *proper size* . . . yes, that was the point. One night in New York a friend of Johnson's took a chance on guessing the real reason for the champion's reluctance to give the Boston Tar Baby his second chance. 'Only one man ever knocked you down, Jack. Only one man, since you became champion. That was Stan Ketchel, a middleweight. It would never do, would it, to be knocked down a second time, by another middleweight?'

Jack Johnson got up and strolled across the drawing-room and looked out of the window at the lights of the harbour. No, he hadn't liked being knocked down by Ketchel; and though defeat from Langford was unthinkable, it had not escaped his imagination that that terrific right hand might have gravelled him as Ketchel had in the past. To be knocked down by another middleweight would have been as humiliating as to be beaten by anyone of his own size. His friend's perception was a bit too sharp.

'Sam McVey was the second best man in my time,' he said. 'The fellow I didn't care to meet was big Sam McVey.'

And there had been some truth in it too. True, McVey had only twice beaten Langford to the four victories Langford could claim over him. True, Jeannette's record against McVey was infinitely more impressive than his record against Little Sambo. But there wasn't any doubt, all the same, that Sam McVey had given Johnson a closer run for his money than either of the other two.

'Let me tell you about McVey,' said Johnson, shutting out the glittering New York night. 'You think Ketchel was tough, and Langford was tough. There never was a tough babby like Sam McVey. None of us Negro boys could find white men to meet us in the first few years of the twentieth century and McVey, more than the others, did most of his fighting abroad. You'll have heard about his fight in Paris with Jeannette. That's boxing history. But maybe it's not so well known that he began in the ring when he was a kid of eighteen, and his first fight was a twenty-rounder, and the guy he picked on to meet in his very first bout of all was me.'

Jack looked back at that night of 27 February 1903. He had already beaten a great hitter in the gigantic Negro, Hank Griffin; he had knocked out Klondike, and out-pointed the tremendous Denver Ed Martin. But magnificent cannon-fodder as these heroes were, they in no way outshone McVey when stripped for battle. He was 5 feet 10½ inches tall, and weighed 205 pounds. He was as hideous as could be, with flattened nose and thick lips. He was no great boxer, having few of the airs and graces of the stylist. But as a fighter he was hard to eclipse. His head was so tough some of the best men in the game had actually, as Willie Lewis claimed, cracked their fists on it. His stomach was like steel—he was one of the admitted exceptions to the popular belief that Negroes did not like being hit in the stomach.

Johnson was particularly conscious of McVey's superb gift of in-destructibility. Somehow he provoked you as champion to abandon defensive tactics and wade into him with stark aggression in your heart. McVey would meet you halfway, and punch it out with you to the bitter end. He had a right hand which was a prodigious weapon. Even in the first decade of the twentieth century, when most good men had to be gradually ground down by sapping punches to point and mark, McVey was good enough to put away all but the best of them with a single right hook to the jaw.

Against Johnson, in his first fight of all, MacVey was to land this stupendous slog in the twelfth round. Jack reeled, and staggered back against the ropes, with McVey hot on his track slamming home

bone-crushing lefts and rights to the ribs. Every loyal Californian
in Hazard's Pavilion in Los Angeles had been on his feet bellowing
for death to Johnson and victory for the son of the State. As a
matter of fact, that was probably as near as McVey ever got to taking
toll of Johnson. The battered figure on the ropes was groggy indeed,
but out of glazing eyes he watched the attack come in and planned a
campaign of milling on the retreat to save his fortune—and his face.
He had just enough strength left to clinch as McVey came forward.
Just enough *nous* left to chatter as McVey tossed in short-arm jabs
as they wrestled across the ring, 'Nice right that, Sam! Pity you
don't carry a punch, boy. If only you could punch, some day you'd
make a fighter.' By the time the referee pulled them apart the crisis
was over; his legs were no longer bent at the hinges. And before
the round was over he was flicking McVey on the nose with his long
left lead, and explaining between grinning lips how the blow could
have been warded off.

By the end of the twentieth round Jack was in command again,
and few at the ringside remembered how nearly the fight had gone
the other way when the referee raised his glove in token of victory.

The two were to meet three times in McVey's first fifteen months
as a fighter, but Sam never got nearer to defeating his greatest rival
than in that first contest; not even in the return match, which took
place a few months later and which McVey also lost on points over
twenty rounds.

McVey's chief opponents included Denver Ed Martin, who in his
second season knocked him out in ten rounds, a defeat Sam took so
much to heart that he seriously contemplated immediate retirement.
Fortunately for boxing he changed his mind and had repeated re-
venges on Martin for his presumption. Other victims included
Frank Craig, the Coffee Cooler, whom he bludgeoned to extinction
in the third round in Paris. There was also Jim Barry, with whom
he shared a liking for Panama, where Barry carelessly wound up his
career by getting involved in a bar-room brawl which terminated in
his murder. Another victim, during a visit to England, was Boer
Rodel, whose pretensions as a White Hope McVey exposed when he
slogged him around the ring for seven rounds before conclusively
draping him over the canvas. English judges were given a couple of
opportunities of seeing McVey in action and comparing his merits
with Langford's. The general impression was that Langford was the
more marvellous performer.

By the time World War I broke out, it was clear to Big Sam that he was never again to figure as a serious rival to Jack Johnson. New blood was wanted in the sport; and the fans were going to lose interest if Jack were superseded on the throne by a boxer with whose every trick and embellishment of style they were familiar; whom they had known for almost as long as they had known Johnson himself; and whom—what is more—they had known as Johnson's inferior. When the title changed hands a new man would be wanted to take it over. The despondent McVey, who had of course saved nothing, made a tour of the lesser known American cities with Langford as his partner, and the two engaged in a number of unconvincing contests which were generally disliked, before retiring to stage their act in South America.

McVey remained in Panama for the final years of the war, returning after the Armistice to go through the motions (all too perfunctorily) with Langford and Harry Wills, who had already beaten him in old age. A few days before Christmas, 1921, Big Sam died of pneumonia in Harlem Hospital. He had lived as he had fought at his peak, handsomely and fast; and after his death the world heard the news that Sam McVey was to be buried in a pauper's grave. Everyone sighed and did nothing—everyone except one man. At the time of McVey's death Jack Johnson hadn't a dollar to bless himself with; but that was a point of no importance whatsoever. A funeral was an important thing—you couldn't let an old friend like McVey be buried without a tombstone to display his merits. Jack Johnson borrowed the money to pay for a real funeral for the man who gave him the hardest fight of his life. Moreover, though he never repaid 'Peggy' Bettinson or honoured his promise to the National Sporting Club, he somehow dug up the money to repay the friend who lent him enough to see Sam McVey buried with honour and dignity.

At the end of his own course, he looked back with pleasure at that deed. 'McVey was the best of all,' he would say, 'you couldn't let old Sam pass away like that.' Then his mind went back to the old days. There was little Langford, with those gorilla-like arms. There was Jeannette, the classic puncher. There was husky Sam McVey. It seemed like yesterday that they had been the best men in the world, and few remembered them now. But if you could turn back the clock, the world would see three great fighters—any of whom might have been champion in almost any age but that he lived in.

XII

✦✦

HE GRABBED THE CONTEST against Moran in 1914 if for no other reason than to keep his hand in. Except for that one little dust-up with Jim Flynn in Las Vegas, which the police had stopped, he hadn't had a fight since the bout with Jeffries four years ago. He was, and he was ready to face it, as gross and out of condition now as Jeff himself had been at Reno. A friend had called in at his training quarters and had been shaken by the monstrous spectacle of the bloated black panther. 'Jack, you certainly look good. Tremendous! Just a little—how shall I say—well, just a little extra condition, haven't you?'

'Plain fat, boy, plain fat. But you back me all the same.'

It was important that his friend's bet didn't go down the drain; all the same, it was going to be difficult to ensure its safety. Moran was a big, chunky fellow from Pittsburgh who had trained as a dentist but had certainly drawn more teeth with his vast right uppercut (known as 'Mary Ann') than he had with the forceps. He had his own story of what happened in the fight with Jack, which he published during Jack's lifetime and which, as far as the present writer knows, has never been categorically denied.

There was, as Moran has it, plenty of trouble in his camp; so much trouble, indeed, that there was no question of Frank's manager being invited to take a seat in the boxer's corner. Moreover, there was so much fear that Frank's seconds could not be trusted to the last syllable in their support for their principal, that Georges Carpentier, the referee, was persuaded to agree to the suggestion that he would only accept a towel thrown into the ring if this token of surrender was cast there by Willie Lewis, Moran's close personal friend. Somehow—and it cannot have been easy in a camp in which practically everybody was not speaking to practically everybody else —Jack got a message through to Frank Moran himself. The message was simple to the point of starkness. Could Mr Johnson have the pleasure of a chat with Mr Moran before they met in the ring?

When they met, Johnson coolly put forward his proposition. The arrangement, as it stood, was that the boxers were to share half the gate; the winner getting sixty per cent, the loser forty per cent of their share. Moran nodded. 'Well,' said Jack, 'there ain't gonna be no fight. There ain't gonna be no sixty per cent. There ain't gonna be no forty per cent for *you*. What do you think of that?'

Moran stared at him. 'You're backing out?' he asked. 'Afraid to take a beating?'

Jack laughed. 'Never mind who's afraid. The question is, who's afraid of losing his share of the purse?'

This was a question to which Moran full well knew the answer. His face showed it.

'What's wrong with you, Frank? What's money anyway?'

The great white fists closed. 'You can't do this to me, Jack. I'll squeal to the press. I'll show you up.'

'Why not, Frank? They'll believe you, maybe. But you won't get your money.'

The scowl on the dentist's face deepened. 'What do I have to do to get it?'

Jack flashed him his golden smile. 'I knew you'd be a sensible boy. The fact is, Frank, I don't feel like fighting just now. Mind you, I'm fit and strong, but—well, put it this way—it so happens I feel kind of lazy. What I'd like is a little healthy exercise, with nothing much at stake. You give me that exercise, say for eight rounds, and then you lie down and take a nice rest. Sign this paper giving me your promise—that way you earn yourself forty per cent of half the gate. The other way you get nothing.'

Moran argued. Moran stormed. The more he fulminated, the wider became the golden smile. Jack would not argue, or discuss the matter. He had stated his terms. If Frank wanted to spin out the conversation, what about a pleasant chat on the philosophy of Herbert Spencer?

In the end Frank shrugged his great shoulders helplessly. 'At least give me time to think it over,' he pleaded. 'You've sprung this on me out of the blue. Give me a couple of hours.'

Jack nodded. 'All right. You go ahead and put in a couple of hours thinking whether you need a satchelful of notes or not. That's all right. Then in two hours' time you meet me here and tell me the answer.' He smiled again as he noted that Frank didn't even slam the door as he went out. A broken man, if ever he'd seen one. . . .

But Frank Moran was not quite finished yet. When he left Johnson he took a taxi to the office of Theodore Vienne who had sunk thousands in promoting the fight. To Vienne he poured out the whole story. There was, as Moran saw it, only one thing to do:

refuse to enter the ring and give the whole story to the Press. Whatever happened now there would always be rumours and a smell.

Old Theodore Vienne didn't agree. Soon enough the crowds would begin to surround the Velodrome d'Hiver: soon enough the taxis of Paris, which in a few weeks' time would be rushing the last reserves of France to the defence of the city, would arrive with their cargoes of women with gleaming shoulders and eyes bright with expectancy of a new thrill, from the heights of Montmartre, from the boulevards, from the cafés of the Left Bank. There never had been such a fight to excite the women! It might be that a new audience had been found for boxing: and for the Vel d'Hiver. And if this fight didn't come off, for any reason, it might be that the old audience for the sport would not easily be found again.

The impresario laid a hand on Moran's shoulders. 'No, no, my boy, we mustn't back out. We must fight.'

'Yes—but how?'

'It's quite simple. I'm going to telephone my lawyer. Oh yes—and the divisional inspector, the head copper of the district.'

To him Moran should dictate a full statement of what he had done before the fight began. After that he was to go back to Johnson and tell him he agreed to his condition and sign the document promising to lie down in the eighth round. Then, with himself safeguarded (to say nothing of Theodore Vienne and his box-office), he was to go into the ring, and as he came out for the first round he was to tell Johnson that the fight was on the level.

This was Vienne's plan and he whirled his arms and bristled and exploded in excited argument until he had persuaded Moran to agree to it. The few thousands Vienne had invested in staging the fight were safe at last; the gate receipts of more than £20,000 wouldn't have to be returned after all.

It was a great crowd that paid up to £15 for a seat on that night of 27 June 1914 at the Vel d'Hiver. There were over three thousand women in the audience, deliciously dressed as for the opera. Gaby Deslys' new ruby bracelet gleamed at the ringside. Mistinguette's long, dark sable coat hid her yet more interesting legs for a long moment.

And then down the aisle to the front row came a figure who distracted everybody's attention from the women. He might have been Johnson's double, if not the reincarnation of the Black Emperor of Haiti in all his Napoleonic swagger and splendour. In the lapel of his tail coat a purple orchid glowed like a sunset; behind him his white secretary staggered, a captive monarch in the train of a Tartar prince, wilting under a mountainous fur coat. Who was he? Nobody knew. Nobody knows to this day. But he drew all eyes as he swaggered to his seat till Johnson slipped between the ropes to flash his golden smile on every white-bosomed girl at the ringside.

A cheer for Johnson: and a cheer for Frank Moran, his blond hair parted in the middle, a solid chunk of White Hope if ever there was one. And the loudest cheer of all for Georges Carpentier, idol of Paris and referee of this world's championship contest. Whoever else was applauding Carpentier, Moran watched his arrival in the ring with no lively satisfaction. He was a novice as third man in the ring; but his was the only name to which Johnson had given his assent. William A. Brady and Eugene Corri had both been suggested and both been ruled out by Johnson.

The sporadic cheers and the expectant rumble swelled into a general surge of thunder: the boxers were haled together now into the centre of the ring by Carpentier. As they shook hands in the white glare of the cinema arc lights, Moran looked Johnson squarely in the eye and said to him: 'Do your best to-night, Jack. This fight is on the level.' There were those at the ringside who swore that Johnson shuddered as he heard the words. It was the old story of Philadelphia Jack O'Brien and Tommy Burns over again.

And now the bell rang, and the fight was on. Johnson skipped from his corner to the centre of the ring and stood there waiting for Moran to lead. When Moran joined him, he refused to give ground; the champion of the world stood there swaying and sparring, content to let Moran lead to him. For a few rounds the fight was gently interesting rather than nerve-racking. Johnson, for all his flabbiness, was quick enough on his feet to slip or side-step Moran's lumbering attacks. He was much the bigger man: an inch and a half taller and some three stone heavier. Though he did little to hint that he had proved himself the greatest fighter in the world, perhaps in history, there was a suggestion that Johnson had power in reserve. He dominated the scene, even if he was content to pad round the ring doing no more than lay a punctual slap on the challenger half a dozen times a round. The crowd watched reverently: no doubt something volcanic was imminent. In the meanwhile, every expert explained to every newcomer within earshot that you needed years of experience to appreciate this sort of scientific display. Several women whimpered ecstatically at the thud of glove upon flesh.

But in the fifth round the fight came to life. Moran led with a ponderous left; Johnson slipped it, came in close and jolted a rigid right forearm into the short ribs. The white man clinched, wrapping his arms round Johnson's heavily muscled biceps. Johnson wrestled free, and wrapped Moran in his bear-like hug. Carpentier, hovering like a butterfly above the battlefield, shouted to the boxers to break. As he heard the words Moran tried to step back, virtuously adhering to the French Federation's rule that fighters should break clean. But Johnson tightened his grip on Moran's neck, and pulling his head down to within reach, unleashed a thunderous uppercut on to his target.

It was the decisive blow of the battle. It cracked Moran's nose as a walnut is crunched under the heel: the gush of blood to his mouth all but choked him as he reeled back out of range. The crowd came to life with the blow. From the start of the fight Moran, the smaller and lighter man, had been its favourite; now that he was the victim of vicious fouling at the hands of the champion grinning and gibbering in his triumph, its indignation was heartening to witness. Its roaring disapproval was hardly stilled by the appearance of a notice-board announcing: '*Johnson has received a warning. Another breach of the rules and he will be disqualified.*'

It is hard to know why, if it was acknowledged that Johnson had committed a serious foul, he was not disqualified forthwith. Certainly the effect of what had been virtually a free-hit was serious enough for Moran. It made breathing a particularly difficult feat for the remaining fifteen rounds of the fight, while more than once the injured fighter found himself literally gagged by his own blood.

But Moran kept pegging on. His courage and his aggression were unflagging. He had his best chance in the seventh round when he tried a 'shift' on the Negro and rammed home his right so heavily that the champion rocked on his heels. Johnson's showmanship, however, came to his rescue almost before his brain was cleared. He stretched forward to pat Moran on the shoulder. 'That's the way, Frankie boy. You work on that punch and get it real good and one day you'll be champion.' The crowd which had wanted his head on a charger five minutes earlier, crowed their appreciation of his clowning.

The eighth round came, and every time Johnson worked Moran into a corner his hopes were high that his evening's stint was nearly over. 'Come on, Frank, *now*!' he would plead; but Frank shook his bloody head and muttered: 'Come on, Jack, come on and fight.'

The battle wore on, stern, relentless and unlit by drama. After

Moran's refusal to lie down in the eighth round Johnson's form improved. The look of slackness disappeared; he went about his work like a tradesman. All the same, as the fight drew to an end, Jack felt weariness creep over him irresistibly. He'd never felt like this before. The last few rounds with Langford or McVey striving to turn the tables at the eleventh hour had been the most exciting part of the affair: the thrill that made the whole unrelaxing routine of a contest worth while, because there was always the outside chance that something might go wrong and the worse man win after all.

Glorious to hold out against those furious assaults in the lonely eyrie of his superiority! Glorious to remain aloof and victorious with the enemy pounding vainly at the gate!

But this time it wasn't like that. He was no master of defence, exposing with airy magic all the sweating efforts of mere humanity to haul him down from his pedestal by sheer brute force. He was a tired old Negro, shuffling around and hoping to keep out of the way of Moran's flamboyant right uppercut. Again and again Frank whirled it home, and again and again Johnson's sense of timing was just good enough to pull his chin out of the danger zone. But as they wrestled together in the eighteenth round he murmured to Frank: 'It's been a nice fight, boy. Let's take it easy from now till the bell'—only to see the white man redouble his efforts to land that slaughterous punch on the point.

The twentieth round at last! A long left lead flipping back the red and white face under the tousled fair hair, still parted in the middle like the hair of a boulevardier after all the sweat and agony its owner had gone through. A little skip and shuffle out of harm's way when the muscle-bound left hook sought the angle of the jaw. The old trick of bringing up a paralysing punch to the biceps as Moran led with his left. All the showmanship of smile and sneer when he managed to make a white fool of Moran; all the unconcern in the world when 'Mary Ann' caught him, too high to be fatal, almost stunningly on the forehead.

Half a minute to go now! Twenty seconds! Ten! The exhausted old feet were forced to skip around the ring like the feet of a young dancer intoxicated with the joys of buoyancy and speed. The happy chuckle was settled like a mask on the face drained of energy.

The bell. . . . And there was Carpentier crossing the ring to raise unhesitatingly the fleshy black arm of the winner. But the champion of the world passed through an almost silent crowd on the way to his dressing-room, whereas Frank Moran was cheered till he was out of sight as if the crown was upon his sweat-drenched head.

Despite the applause for Moran, few serious-minded citizens disagreed with Carpentier's verdict. One who did was A. G. ('Smiler') Hales, at that time boxing critic on a London paper. By the Smiler's reckoning, Moran was the winner by a wide margin of points. It should, however, be pointed out that Hales was not an invariable admirer of Carpentier: when the Frenchman knocked out Kid Lewis while the latter was still eyeing the referee for instructions, Hales was the most indignant of the many angry spectators. 'So much then,' he declared, 'for France's vaunted chivalry.'

Defeat was not the bitterest memory of the fight that Frank Moran was to take back to Pittsburgh. There was the little matter of his share of the purse—the forty per cent of half the gate of $40,000 for which Frank had fought so bravely inside the ring and out of it. Someone had tipped him off to get up early in the morning to call at the office for his 8,000 francs. Frank took the tip, but he didn't get up early enough. Johnson was before him, and had scooped the kitty. Moreover, by the mysterious processes of French law there seemed to be no chance of redress, short of bringing Johnson before the French courts in a civil action. So Frank's share of the world's championship fight must be written down as experience—no more. He even had to pay for medical attention to his broken nose, unless Parisian doctors of that age treated American dentists for nothing, which on the face of it seems unlikely.

For Paris, the contest, even though the boxing was rarely spectacular, was the great event of a splendid season. The takings and the attendance at the Vel d'Hiver that night remained records for many years to come. As for the glamour and drama of that brilliant occasion on the eve of the first salvos of the Great War—nothing like it had been known since the Duchess of Richmond's Ball in the small hours before the trumpets sounded for Waterloo.

But if Paris cheered and Frank Moran fumed, Jack Johnson was left with a scowl of perplexity on his clearly marked features as he discussed the future with Gus Rhodes and Lucille the night after the fight. It was no good trying to cheer him up by reminding him that Moran was rated (perhaps next to Gunboat Smith) as the leading White Hope of the world. It was no good hoping to reassure him with assertions that everyone—except 'Smiler' Hales, whose influence on world opinion was not paramount—agreed that he had beaten Moran emphatically enough. Jack knew, better than any of those who were near to him, the significance of the fight and its result. That night at the Vel d'Hiver he was where Jim Jeffries had been at Reno; and he was lucky there was no Jack Johnson in the prime of life waiting for him in the opposite corner.

It wasn't only that he was slower and less terrible in execution than he had been at his peak; under-training could have explained all that. But the fact was—the fact that only he knew with the certitude of one who has analysed his own instincts—he hadn't the cold fury at heart any more. The hate of the subject race no longer narrowed his eyes and flared his nostrils: the devilish pride to peacock it above all men no longer possessed him like a phobia. Those were the gifts that had lifted him above the ruck; success had mellowed him so that he had lost them. Now he was just a fighter like any other; endowed with exceptional gifts but without the magic that made him invulnerable.

Well, he had given the white race the lesson it needed. He had fed on his hate and grown fat as an emperor. Also, he was thirty-six years old; no man should be asked to fight at that age. He had—to-night anyway—money enough and fame enough to last him a lifetime. It was his task to retire, as Jeff had retired, but having learned the lesson that there must be no come-back.

And yet he revolted against such a plan. His hatred might be dulled, his fantastic vainglory sated, but he still felt an immediate contempt for his neighbour that quickly flowered into pugnacity; he still swelled with a natural arrogance which demanded that he should concede himself inferior to no man in the world.

XIII

◆◆◆

THE SUNLIGHT made the Strand dance in the heat haze. The paper boys selling their halfpenny *Stars* and *News* stood at the corners fanning themselves with their wares. The fat old lady with the huge basket of roses outside Gatti's was as wilted as her own Gloire de Dijons. Jack strolled jauntily down the street. This weather suited him. He grinned his golden grin as he remembered Klondike, who had earned his nickname because he was the only Negro who could fight his best in the snow. He was no Klondike. Sunshine for him! The heat haze over the Texas wheatfields. The sweltering streets of Chi—the broiling tenements of Harlem with the kids fighting each other to get into the spray from the watercart.

London in August for him! True, he was barred from fighting in the town, but anyway where were the boxers who could bring him out in a healthy sweat? He remembered the row there'd been, several years before, when they'd wanted him to fight that white marble Apollo, Billy Wells. The churches, the police, the Home Secretary—oh, my goodness, the whole of Britain, short of the King, was in arms against that little proposal. And now poor old Billy was still champion, but no one would suggest he should tangle with L'il Arthur. No, sir—not while he knew what was good for him!

He stopped outside Gatti's. Bessie, the fat flower-woman, held up a bunch of roses in a dripping hand. 'No good,' he said. 'How could I give 'em to Lucille? They're dead as cabbages. Give us an orchid.'

He was wearing his biscuit silk suit, a pale golden trilby, and the fine new shoes of crocodile and doeskin. A big purple orchid would just set him off.

' 'Aven't no orchid, mister,' Bessie began to whine. 'These 'ere camellias are all the go.'

'An orchid, Bessie. A great big purple one. One pound for an orchid.'

'The Duke of Devonshire's wearing these camellias.'

'He can afford to.'

Bessie shouted incomprehensibly at a guttersnipe who darted off through the heat haze towards the flower-stall outside Charing Cross station. 'Two minutes, guv'nor—and no extra charge.'

A policeman joined the group. 'Good afternoon, Mr Johnson. Saw your show down at the Elephant the other night. Proper caution, I reckon.'

The golden smile was as good as a pat on the back.

'That dance of your wife's—the Oyster Shell dance—my goodness, that was great.'

'Lucille's a clever girl. I don't think *Seconds Out's* a bad show at all.'

The guttersnipe was in sight with a purple orchid of sorts.

'Mr Johnson,' said the policeman, still with his smile and without changing the tone of his voice, 'I came up to warn you. You're being followed.'

'Followed!'

'Yes, sir. On the other side of the road. I been watching the chap all the while you been talking to Bessie, here. He's tailing you all right.'

Jack put the orchid in his buttonhole. 'A sovereign for you, Bessie. And a dollar for you, boy.' He shook the policeman by the hand. 'Thanks, son, thanks a lot. There's no reason in the wide world any man should tail me. But thanks all the same.'

Back stage at the theatre he ran into the manager talking to a Senator from the South he hadn't seen since the Jeffries fight. Oh, well, one should always be polite.

'Good evening to you, Senator.'

'Don't talk to me, you God-damned nigger.'

Jack still smiled, but his quiet drawl had an edge to it as he turned to the manager: 'Do you allow your stars to be talked to this way?'

The manager shrugged his shoulders. 'It don't matter to me what way he talks to you. The way I hear it, a lot of people are talking rough to you now.'

'The best news I had yet,' said the Senator.

'Get out,' said Jack. His voice was hardly above a whisper, but his nostrils flared and his fingers clenched as he spoke.

The Senator laughed. 'It's not me that's getting out,' he sneered. 'Show him the nice new contract you got for him, mister.'

The manager flung open the door of his office. A tall wooden-faced man with detective written all over him, stood up to face the group.

'Are you Mr Jack Johnson?'

The clenched fist resolved itself into fingers again. 'What do you think? Do I look like Snow White?'

'Sure he's Jack Johnson,' said the Senator. 'Daren't show his face in any State of the Union. The fighting champion!' He spat the end of a fresh cigar on to the crocodile and doeskin shoes.

'I take it you are Mr Jack Johnson,' said the detective.

'Take it, then. It's all yours.'

'It is my duty to inform you,' said the wooden-faced man in his wooden voice, 'that I am to serve on you this order to leave the country within twenty-four hours.'

'*What?* What the hell——'

'I'm afraid I've nothing more to say to you, sir. Those are my orders, and I've carried them out.'

The detective opened the door and went out into the passage. Jack was after him in a flash.

'But good God, man—what's it all about? Leave England in twenty-four hours? What have I ever done to have to leave England at all?'

The detective hesitated. When he took his wooden face off at the end of a day's work he mightn't be a bad sort of fellow at all: the sort of man who'd want to know how hard Fitz could hit, and would take a pride in passing it on to all the chaps at the station next day.

'Listen, sir,' he said at last, 'I don't know what it's all about. I only know one thing. You got enemies here in this country.'

'*Enemies!* But what am I to do?'

'That I couldn't tell you. But if you got friends too—big men—well, sir, this is the time to call 'em in. Good day to you, sir.'

Out in front the audience were getting impatient. He could hear the call, 'Good old Jack!' echoing from beyond the stage through the offices and corridors. He stepped on to the stage. 'Good old England!' he shouted, and the cheering swelled resoundingly. A little step-dance across the stage, a little humming and then loud and clear: 'It's a Long Way to Tipperary.' The crowd took up the haunting chorus thunderously.

At the show's end he found that Lucille refused to treat the story seriously. 'We've done nothing and no Ku Klux Klanner's got any pull over here,' she said. 'To-morrow we'll go to the biggest big shots we know and get this thing straightened out. And now come home. I'm going to cook you Chicken Maryland. I guess you need it.'

She pushed open their front door.

'Jack! For God's sake, Jack!'

He went past her into their living-room. The lights were on; the windows overlooking the street wide open. The gold flower vase still stood in the centre of the table. Lucille's gold and ivory cigarette-holder lay on a side table, beside the onyx ash-tray. But through the open door into their bedroom he could see the trunks, piled against the wall. Someone had opened them; someone had flung out the suits and silk shirts he hadn't bothered to unpack.

He stood, looking ruefully down at the confusion on the bedroom floor. Half a dozen silk suits—pale blue and peacock blue, white and silver—tangled in a heap. The diamond bracelet he'd given Lucille last birthday lay on the little mound made by her black lace nightdresses. His shoes and crested pyjamas were strewn over the floor. The four volumes of Herbert Spencer and the volume of Edmund Spenser he'd bought by mistake had been ripped apart and leaves and covers were scattered round the room, so that it looked like the start of a paper chase.

He knelt to search, and looked up at Lucille. 'Nothing's gone, honey. It's all here, your necklaces, my emerald stickpin—everything.'

'No one came here for nothing.'

He had never seen her look so terror-stricken. Her face had the blank look of the faces of the doomed he had seen years ago in Galveston on the night of the tidal wave.

'No,' he said, 'no one came here for nothing.' He turned over his silk vests, his pile of satin ties, the Charvet shirts with his monogram on the left breast. He couldn't count them, because he had no idea to the nearest dozen how many he might have; but they seemed all right.

'Something's gone,' he said at last. 'The packet of papers George Thomas gave me in Moscow. The packet he said never to let get into the hands of the Germans.'

Lucille sat in the chair by the open window. 'He said they were copies of notes between the Czar and the Kaiser,' she remembered. 'I always thought that was George's big talk. Now I wonder.'

Jack straightened. He began to kick the piles of clothes into a single heap. 'George didn't have to talk big. He *was* big. Remember how he lived. Who he saw.'

She remembered the nights in Moscow, the parties where the Grand Dukes clanked and dazzled. The shadow of Rasputin at a moonlit party in the garden. 'But the Czar and the Kaiser . . .' she said weakly.

Jack shrugged his shoulders. 'All he asked was that we should keep them for him, till we met again. And we've failed him. I should have given them over to someone to guard. The police maybe, if the police here aren't politicians.'

'Yes,' she said bitterly, 'and the way it looks to me is the police have helped themselves.'

He stared at her.

'Yesterday,' she said, 'no one knew about these papers. To-day someone finds them. And what happens since they're found? The Senator bawls you out, the theatre manager spits on you, the police order you out of England. What was in those papers that was so damn' important?'

He could have kicked himself for never having looked. True, he'd promised George never to break the seals, but he could have invented any old lie to explain that. And now—well, what *had* happened now?

'What do you think, Lucille?' he said helplessly.

But she didn't know either. All she could say was that they might as well have their Chicken Maryland anyway. And to-morrow he must go to Hiram Maxim and ask him to help them. Sir Hiram was always saying he was their friend, and admired Jack more than anyone, next to Basil Zaharoff. Long before he'd been the great inventor of machine guns, Hiram had been a boxer too; and in some part of his mind there flourished a boy's reverence for the man who had become champion at the sport in which he had only served an apprenticeship.

But Hiram couldn't help. The Government wouldn't listen to him; he had no political influence anywhere. 'Why don't you go to Lonsdale?' was the best that he could suggest.

And Lord Lonsdale, though his cordial reception raised Jack's morale to fighting pitch, couldn't really help either. In his drawing-room in Carlton House Terrace he had stood beside his great Borzoi and smoked his enormous cigar and talked blandly of Peter Jackson, the finest fighter who ever lived, in his lordship's opinion. 'For his sake alone, I'd do anything I could to help you, Johnson. And of course I will. But these are difficult times. A country gets hysterical when it's fighting for its existence.'

'But me, your lordship—what would I have to do with the war?'

'I don't know, Johnson. I don't know. But you've been in

Russia. You've come from Germany. A mystery man!' He fondled the Borzoi's imperious, stupid head. 'Lovely creatures, aren't they, Johnson? But not as beautiful as Jackson stripped for action that day he beat Slavin.'

The footman in the canary livery of the Lowthers, brought Jack's coat. For a moment he wondered whether he had been wise to have it lined with silver and violet silk. But Lord Lonsdale took it, from the footman's hands. 'Allow me to help you, Johnson.'

'And what would you advise me to do, my lord?'

'See your solicitor. Tell him the truth—whomever else you tell, well, anything else. See him at once, to-night, this afternoon, without fail.'

'Thank you, my lord.'

The senior partner looked at his finger nails—there seemed nowhere else to look. 'All I can advise you is that if you fight this order, there's a good chance you may succeed, if you've told me the whole truth. I say, you *may*. But I don't know who has these papers you've lost, or what they consist of. All I know is the Home Office, because of the papers, or because of what some enemy who has stolen them, has told them, doesn't consider you a welcome visitor to England at this moment.'

Jack's awed eyes travelled round the room. He took in the tiers of faded leather-bound volumes, the enormous pewter inkstand on the senior partner's desk, the pile of parchment tied with pink ribbon in the tray beside him. The old man was looking away from his parchment finger tips at last, looking at him with beady lizard's eyes out of his parchment cheeks.

'You don't believe me, sir,' he said sadly.

'Mr Johnson, I never disbelieve a client until I'm forced to. But somebody at the Home Office wouldn't believe you. Somebody in high authority. No'—as Jack started to speak—'nobody who has had his mind made up for him by a prejudiced Southern Senator. Somebody who has seen these documents, which I haven't; somebody who knows just what information you have been carrying in your baggage.'

'Which I don't,' Jack pointed out.

'So you tell me. You would have to convince the Home Office of that fact, which might be difficult to do as your friend Thomas seems to have disappeared for the time being. Moreover you won't get much help from the Russian Embassy. All they know is that when you went to an army barracks in Moscow, you got your orders to leave Russia at once, because you were a friend of Thomas.'

'I see. So I must leave England too—because I'm a friend of Thomas, whom you never heard of.'

'The Russians are our allies and friends, and we are fighting a war. You cannot expect our Home Office to welcome you in the circumstances.'

'Then I must go.'

The senior partner drummed his fingers on blotting paper that showed the spidery writing of a bygone age. 'Or prove yourself innocent. The onus is on you.'

Jack got up. The old books, the parchment quires in their pink ribbons, the tall panelled room—how could a man live against such a background and know which way the world spun round? He said: 'Thank you, sir, for your advice. How much do I owe you?'

'My clerk will send you a bill.'

Jack fished with rehearsed carelessness in the pocket of his jacket. 'I like to pay as I go along. Will this cover me?' He dug out a handful of hundred pound notes and dropped one on the pile of parchment.

The senior partner put on his spectacles, held the note up to the light. Then he unlocked the drawer of his desk and counted out nine ten pound notes. From his vest pocket he produced a sovereign purse, from which he took six golden sovereigns. Finally from his trousers pocket he counted six half-crowns, a shilling and two sixpences. 'As you like, Mr Johnson. Here is your change.'

Jack laughed. He could not boast he had won that particular contest on points. 'And now, sir, I've had your advice. You tell me I've got to prove my innocence. And I can't. So I suppose the law is—I get out of England by to-morrow?'

The senior partner sniffed expressively. He dined with the Home Secretary twice a year, and by the end of dinner generally summoned up courage to call him by the nickname he had used at school.

'Well, sir, I'll tell you what I aim to do. I'm going. I don't reckon to stay in any country that doesn't welcome me, or my wife. But I'm going in my own time. Be so kind as to tell them *that*, next time you meet the gentlemen who run the law here.'

All the same, when he went out into the street he felt that the policeman on the corner was looking at him as if he was something else besides the world's champion. He felt there were eyes in ambush watching him as he walked like a peacock down the Strand, or wrapped the tigerskin rug over his knees when he got into the De Dion.

And a week afterwards the men in ambush came out into the open as he made his way home down Shaftesbury Avenue after a gambling party in the small hours. There were half a dozen of them, a couple of them scouting to keep the coast clear at the street corner. The first thug came at him from out of the doorway of a bookshop with a wild swing which he had learned to dodge in the long ago when he sparred with Walcott, training for Scaldy Bill. As the swing went over his top hat and his counter crashed home to the mark, the second man jumped into the open and tried back-heeling him into the gutter. Jack slipped the rush, up-ended him, and was quick enough to hit him with a right cross before he bounced off the pavement.

Two more of them were coming on—and still not a policeman in sight! For a fleeting second a wild terror touched him: who was on his side in this country? Then the savage joy of combat gripped him as it had gripped him so often in the past. He was as happy as he had been slamming away Langford's huge leads, or counter-punching against Frank Childs. He sent over a great indestructible right and rejoiced as it thudded against the jaw.

Almost simultaneously he felt a blow on his cheek that was more cruel than Fitz's mighty mule-kick of a punch. He tasted the gushing blood against his tightened lips, and knew that the man retreating down the street had slashed at him with the metal end of a heavy belt. By a miraculous inch the blow had missed his eye—he was still on his feet and carrying the fight to his man. As he went after him, he saw the scouts at the street corners melt into the distance; he heard the cheep of police whistles.

He stood his guard, his brain in a whirl, as the gang ran for its life and his preservers gathered round him. So he was not alone, after all. The forces of law and order were still on his side. Well and good! But in his heart of hearts he was sorry to be rescued. It was good to be standing with his back to the wall again, beating down impossible odds. Born and bred in a Battle Royal, sirs—born and bred in a Battle Royal!

But that night when he told Lucille what had happened (you couldn't explain away a gashed cheek as the result of a friendly argument about a busted flush), she gripped him as if he had never been meant to battle for his place in the sun.

'You've got other friends besides the police, darling. Jack Curley is coming—with a proposition!'

Jack Curley! That old friend was always brimming with ideas to bring him back into the ring. He'd been over in the States ever since the Moran fight in Paris, figuring out a way of luring the world's champion back to defend his title in his home-land. Curley was just the boy to do the trick! He had found himself a couple of theatrical angels too, in Lawrence Waber and Harry Frazee. He had the money to put up to make it worth Johnson's while to fight again. He had influence with the champion too.

XIV

◆◆◆

As soon as he arrived in England Jack Curley invited Jack and
Lucille to dine with him. There was a spray of orchids by Lucille's
place at the table: a good start to an evening of negotiation with Jack.
They had finished their *poulet à la Bresse* before Curley came to the
point.

'Jack, my boy, you're wasting your time in England. They won't
let you fight here, and you're no good at all unless you're fighting.'

Jack played with the *Bombe Alaska*. He wondered how much
Curley knew. Probably everything—he was that sort of man. Still,
there was no harm in stringing him along. 'I like it here, Curley.
They're friendly folk, the English. I got plenty of dough. What's
the fun in having your guts whaled out when you don't have
to?'

Curley signalled for more champagne. From below the window
of the blacked-out room you could hear the hoot of a launch on the
moonlit Thames. 'You know what they're calling you in the States.
The non-fighting champion. How do you like that?'

Jack laughed softly. 'Suits me. The word that matters is champion. Who do they think can beat me this time? Is it Sam Langford
again?'

A waiter brought brandy and cigars. Jack tried to kid Lucille to
smoke a small Henry Clay. Curley walked over to the window and
looked down on the silvery Thames.

'Not Langford, Jack. Everyone knows you'll never fight the Tar
Baby again, whatever your reasons may be.'

Jack leant back and crossed his feet on the tablecloth. 'There is
neither gold nor glory to be gained by me in fighting Langford
again.'

'Not by you, perhaps, but perhaps by Langford.'

Lucille had refused the small cigar, but accepted a cigarette, for
smoking the like of which a lady of irreproachable character had
that week been evicted from the public lounge on the appeal of outraged stockbrokers at neighbouring tables. Now she flung the violet-
tipped butt into the night and pulled the curtains together. 'Look
here, Curley,' she exclaimed, 'you haven't come all the way from

New York to try to taunt Jack to get sore at Sam Langford. That's been tried before. You've got a proposition—or thank you for the nice dinner and we've all been wasting our time.'

Curley came back to the table and patted Lucille's bare shoulder like a proud schoolmaster. He had always known how far he could go with Jack. 'Right you are,' he said. 'So I've got a proposition. I've got a new heavyweight. *Now* are you interested, Jack Johnson, my boy?'

Jack poured himself out a little brandy; then seeing that Lucille's eyes were on Curley, he doubled the dose. 'A new heavyweight . . .' He sighed like a disappointed lover. 'These new heavyweights have a way of being old heavyweights brought out again to buy themselves a little new business. Let's see now—it wouldn't be Flynn or Jim Johnson. It wouldn't be Denver Ed or Jeannette. Nor Moran again. I give up, Curley; I never was no good at conundrums.'

The waiter arrived with fresh coffee. Curley made a great show of not saying a word a spy could pick up until he had gone again. Then he carefully chose a cigar, pierced it with the air of a surgeon conducting a major operation, and spoke at last with the first smoking-ring.

'What do you say to a cowboy, Jack, a damn' great hunk of cowboy? Six foot six inches of him, a freak that'd drag the world in to watch him even if he couldn't fight for peanuts.'

Jack's eyes glittered. 'And can he fight for peanuts?'

'Peanuts won't be what we'll be offering him.'

The golden smile gleamed in the dusk across the table. 'Nor me, I hope.'

'Nor the champion of the world.'

Jack held his brandy against the moonlit window, and drained it at a gulp. 'I can lick any damn cowboy and knock cold any damn steer on the range,' he said. 'I could kill them, if I'd the mind. The only man in the world who'd have a chance with me is Sam McVey, and I could punch the tripes out of old Sam's guts if I got me trained for the job. What's his name, this cowboy?'

'He's called Jess Willard.'

'Who's he ever beaten? Did he whip McVey?'

'He did not. He never fought him that I heard.'

Jack blew smoke among the candle flames. 'Listen, Curley,' he said, 'last time we talked business the plan was for me to defend my title in Buenos Aires. I reckoned I might settle down there for life, and I still reckon I might. Whoever I was to fight for you down in

South America, it wasn't Jess Willard. However, I can beat a cowboy as well as anyone else. How's that suit you?'

Curley was just a little too quick to agree to everything. 'All I wanted, Jack, was to sound you as to what you felt about this Willard.'

He came over to Jack and put his arms about him. 'Good God, when I remember all the trouble I had with you a couple of years back. But look at the two of you now! I'll say it was worth it.'

Lucille pressed his arm. 'We're grateful to you, Curley. We always will be. But . . .' she sighed.

'Well?'

'I don't know. It seems kind of sad. Why does this have to be the Thames—what has Jack done so that he shouldn't look out on the Hudson River?'

'I reckon he has a right to.'

They were silent for a while, till Jack muttered, 'I can lick any damn cowboy on earth,' and kicked at the ice bucket.

Curley began to talk of old friends. Philadelphia Harry Lewis was doing nicely thank you; Bunny Barton was playing the horses and had bought himself a tobacco farm. Poor old Dixie Kid was hanging out at some gym up in Liverpool and not eating all that much. And suddenly Curley put a hand on Jack's arm. 'How's your mother, Jack? The last I heard the news wasn't good, wasn't good at all. They told me the old lady was pretty bad.'

Jack shook his head. He couldn't find a voice to tell what he was frightened of.

'Wouldn't you like to see her again?'

'*Like* to!' said Lucille. 'It's all Jack wants to do in life.'

'You know that, Curley,' Jack murmured. 'I'd take all the prison they've planned for me in the States just to see her again for an hour. But what's the use? It would break her heart if they took me, and they sure would.'

Curley's eye was glittering across the candle-lit table. His big moment had come. 'Jack,' he said so softly the boxer had to lean forward to follow him, 'I've got a plan. It's possible there's a way you can fight again, earn yourself a few thousand bucks, get yourself a pardon—and have your mother beside you for the evening of her life.'

'Curley, if you've really got a plan, tell me. But if you're just stringing me on I'll bash you the way I bashed Langford.'

He saw his little mother now, wanting him, waiting for him to

play her 'Coming for to carry me home' on the old giant viol he'd
bought back from the north twenty years ago. She'd have changed
so much in two or three years. He tried to imagine the change, to
see her as she must be now. All he could think of was that she must
be smaller than ever; his little doll would have shrunk so that she
needed protection more than ever in the big world so full of enemies.

'Yes, Jack, I've got a plan. You'll fight this Willard—but not in
B.A. Somewhere nearer home; say Mexico City. That fight'll
draw every real fan all the way from New York.'

'How does that fight help me to see my mother again?'

Curley knew that the crucial moment was coming: the split
second when Johnson's future was determined, for good or evil.
'Listen, Jack, when you fight Willard, one of two things will happen.
Either you'll win, in which case, you see to it that you win well, so
that every sport from the States is proud to have you for an American.
Or—well—or the fight goes the other way.'

Lucille had never taken her eyes from Curley's face. 'All right,
Curley. So Jack either wins or loses. So then what?' She saw his
hand shake as he poured himself brandy before answering.

'Why is the Government out for Jack's blood?' he said at last.
'Because Jack's the boss of all the white men. Because the whole
damn lot of them have to kiss the ground before him. But suppose
Jack loses. He's nothing then, nobody. No government will be out
to humble a has-been.'

Jack went to the window and held his fingers to the moonlight so
that the big diamond in his ring gleamed like blue flame. 'Correct,
Curley. But what happens if I win? Had you considered the possibility that I might win?'

'Of course you'll win. I only put the worst case to you first, so you
shouldn't think I'm holding out on you.'

'Very well then, I win. And I win high, wide and handsome.
What happens next?'

This was it. He either took the bait or refused it. You could read
the crisis in Curley's eyes.

'A pardon, Jack. A pardon happens then. All the time I've been
home I've been working for one, and I reckon it's possible I'll get it
all sewed up.'

'You reckon?'

'Here are the letters, Jack; you read them.'

In silence Jack read through the sheets, passing each letter as he
finished it over to Lucille. Curley watched them anxiously. None

of the letters promised a pardon; none of them said a pardon was impossible. The subject was under discussion. You just couldn't tell what was going to happen.

Jack took the letters back from Lucille, folded them carefully and put them on the table. He said nothing; his face was a mask. It was Lucille who spoke. 'What's the alternative, Jack?'

Yes, that was the point. What was the alternative? He must quit England. He must go somewhere. Back to Paris, to lose all resemblance to a champion, to swagger around the boulevards, gross and enfeebled, failing in the divine force that marked him out from other men, till in the end some young buck called his bluff and gave him no alternative but to exhibit himself as the sham he was. Or to chuck the ring for good: he was in his later thirties, at an age when most fighters had given the world all they'd got to give. But he remembered others. Fitz, bald and barrel-chested, who'd never been given his chance until he'd reached an age when most men had given up. He couldn't give in where Fitz had fought on.

And yet he'd give in to-morrow, he'd lie down on the floor and let some poor dub not worth spitting on take the title from him, if it meant he could get a pardon and a ticket to Texas.

What's the alternative, Jack? He looked round at Lucille. 'You say, do it—fight this Willard in Mexico?'

'Why not? Curley may be right. Then if you lose, you win; and if you win, anyway'll you be no worse off than you are now.'

They were both watching him now. He wondered whether they'd talked it over beforehand, whether they'd rehearsed this scene together. Lucille wanted to get back to the States. Curley wanted—what? Business certainly: perhaps a new heavyweight champion for whom he could promote fights without difficulty anywhere in the world.

Jack stared suspiciously from one to the other. He'd show them. He'd play the game their way—and chop this Willard down as he came. Only—what happened then to his hopes of seeing his mother? Once again his eyes scanned their faces, seeking to read their minds.

Then his hand went out and he drew a long cigar from the box on the table. Curley's smile stiffened. If there was any symbolism in the act, it wasn't the gesture of a man renouncing the flesh for a defence of the title. But you could never tell with Jack Johnson. Before the ash had fallen from his half-smoked cigar and before anyone else had spoken, he had held out his hand to Curley: 'Anyone you like, Jack. And anywhere you like in the world.'

Who was Jess Willard anyway? About the one thing that Jack knew about him was that he was big. He was, in fact, the biggest man in the ring at that time: six feet six inches tall, with a reach of eighty-three inches, generally scaling 250 pounds at the weigh-in. His early career was not exactly distinguished. He had fought no-decision fights with Arthur Pelkey and Luther McCarthy (the latter of whom Jack considered to have been the best of the White Hopes), and a couple of years back had lost a points decision to Gunboat Smith, on which occasion he had been hooted out of the ring as a tribute to his apathetic display.

There were two stories about Willard that Jack liked to chuckle over, though you couldn't be sure he believed them both. The big cow-puncher from Pottawatomie County, Kansas, was said to have early ambitions to become a boxer, though he didn't have his first professional fight till he was twenty-seven. One day he visited a training camp and persuaded the trainer in charge to allow him to spar to show his paces. You see, Jess was absolutely sure that he had the makings of a champion. He knew it, knew it in his heart. The trainer looked at the monster incredulously and laughed his unin-hibited laugh. In the end, however, he was persuaded to allow the giant to spar a few rounds with a chunky welterweight: what was 100 pounds between them?

The spar didn't last long. The welterweight came thundering in and landed a severe cuff with one of his eight-ounce gloves on Jess's midriff. Exit Jess, roaring. The trainer bellowed after him: 'Hey, come back! Didn't you tell me you were going to be a fighter, some day?' As he vanished over the horizon, Jess shouted back: 'So I am. But not *this* day.'

That was the story. Jack didn't believe it, but it was certainly good for a belly laugh.

The other story was certainly true, and grimmer. Once again, Willard was the mug. Way back in 1913, six months after the Gun-boat Smith match, Willard was scheduled to fight Boer Rodel in Milwaukee. Now it so happened that in his previous fight Willard had killed his opponent, Bull Young, in the ring with a tremendous uppercut, from which Young never regained consciousness. Rodel's manager, Jimmy (Man of a Few Million Words) Johnston, Liver-pool-born and sometimes known as the Boy Bandit, knew all about what had happened to Bull Young. Just before the contest began, Johnston went over to examine Willard's gloves. As he did so, he muttered to the giant: 'Easy on him with that big right of yours.'

Willard retorted, as well he might: 'What the hell do you mean?' but —since example is insidious—he kept his voice as low as a conspirator's. 'I mean,' said the Boy Bandit, 'his heart is bad. One full-scale smash in this fight, and he's a dead Boer.'

Willard recoiled. 'What's he fighting for?'

'Money. The usual thing. His wife and kids need feeding.'

Willard muttered angrily: 'My manager shouldn't have fixed me up with such a fight.'

The Boy Bandit smiled winsomely. 'What's it got to do with him? Nuttin'! He don't get tried for manslaughter when anything goes wrong.'

Soon enough the bell went for the first round. Rodel was scared, but not half as scared as Willard. Once or twice he hauled off to launch a great smash to the jaw or ribs, but always his eye seemed to light on Jimmy Johnston sitting there at the ringside, tapping his heart significantly with his forefinger. By the time the fight was half-way through, Willard was going through the motions like a sleep-walker and Rodel was waltzing into action like a general who enjoys dictating his terms to an enemy on the run. At the end of the no-decision bout, most spectators thought Rodel had shared the honours, and Willard's stock as a White Hope had slumped.

But that was not good enough for Rodel. Flushed with success, the Boer demanded a return match.

The Boy Bandit shook his head. 'Far from wise,' he opined, but Rodel was insistent, and at last Johnston allowed himself to be persuaded. This time Willard decided to give Rodel's heart a real work-out, and with a nod and a smile to Johnston he set about his man as if he had two old scores to pay. He won on a knock-out in the ninth round.

Good stories—and somehow they didn't suggest that the Potta-watomie giant was a killer. Still, he had done pretty well in the last three years for a man who was lazy and had to be pushed and bullied by his new manager, Tom Jones, into fighting for a living.

Certainly no one who was watching boxing at the time Willard was at the top of the tree considered him a world-beater. He wasn't in the class of Luther McCarthy, who had died in the ring in the first minute of his fight with Pelkey; or of Pelkey himself, who never got over that terrible day in Calgary, never thereafter won a fight, and died within a few years of sleeping sickness. Edward J. Smith (called Gunboat because of the size of his feet) was a heavyweight with a finer record than Willard—he had beaten Moran and Pelkey,

Rodel and Jim Flynn—but they passed him over in favour of the giant. Al Palzer of Iowa had looked like a good prospect too, with victims in Tom Kennedy (the Millionaire Boxer), Billy Wells and Al Kaufman. But just before the war Al's form had gone all to pieces, in two senses of the words—for not only had he been defeated by three of his four opponents, but he had also quarrelled with his father, who had shot him dead on the spot.

No one reckoned Jim Flynn as any great shakes. Hadn't he been knocked out by Stanley Ketchel, the middleweight, in three humiliating rounds? The greatest victory of his career, the one-round knock-out of Jack Dempsey, was still hidden in the womb of time; and even when it occurred it was to leave no impression whatever on the connoisseurs of the period.

Bombardier Wells, whom Johnson hadn't been allowed to fight way back in 1911, remained the best boxer among all the challengers, even if he completely lacked the temperament for the rough-and-tumble. But you couldn't have put Wells forward as a serious contender: Palzer, Carpentier and Gunboat Smith had all put him away, even if he had shown each of them something of the airs and graces of boxing before the climax. It wasn't that Wells couldn't hit. He hit Iron Hague harder than Langford had hit him, according to the man on the receiving end. He hit Palzer so hard that his glove burst open, and Palzer turned a back-somersault, to crash on his face. But Wells was pitiful and had no heart to finish off a battered and bleeding opponent, and that was why it was Willard whom Curley had chosen to meet Jack for his title in Mexico City, or anywhere else on the map.

At that, it wasn't going to be so easy to get the fight arranged to suit everyone. Jack Curley, relying on Jack's handshake, immediately returned to America with the mission of concluding financial arrangements to stage the contest in Mexico City. He believed that the President himself would welcome the event. It would put Mexico City on the map of the world as the Jeffries fight had put Reno on the map; and as, years later, the Tunney-Gibbons fight was supposed to draw the attention of the universe to Selby, Nevada.

But Curley's calculations were upset by a circumstance against which any business man of the period with commitments in Mexico would normally have insured himself. Revolution brought Mexico into the public eye before the Willard-Johnson fight could be scheduled to do the trick. The President fled to Tampico; and Pancho Villa, the new leader, was frightened of allowing a contest to be staged under his rule which was fraught with so many international complications.

Curley's next move was a bold bluff. His press campaign urged on his home public that every red-blooded American was eager to see the fight that Mexico hadn't the courage to stage. Why not put it on at El Paso, Texas? The public seemed agreeable, but no amount of lobbying could get an assurance from the politicians that Johnson could return to Texas without incurring immediate arrest.

Meanwhile Jack and Lucille had torn up their roots in Europe and arrived on the Mexican border. More than once the champion had driven up to the frontier to try the effect of the golden smile on the United States Marshal, only to be told that the one way he would be allowed to cross was in the character of a fugitive from justice returning to surrender. There were moments when Jack was ready to shrug his shoulders and give in. He had had a long, wearisome chase round the world in search of a fight he wasn't much interested in anyway.

In the end, he went with Curley to Havana, Cuba, and there at last the great fight was scheduled to take place on Monday, 5 April 1915.

XV

✦✦✦

IT WAS A BROILING DAY. It was a queer thing, whenever he had put
the championship at stake it had always been blazing weather. He
had beaten Burns on a day it was a pity to waste out of the Pacific.
He had beaten Jeffries on a roasting afternoon when the 'forty-
niners wished they were clean-shaven. Now in Havana it was
weather to dry out cigars in.

By a quarter to two (New York time) the fighters were in the
open-air ring. There wasn't any question of the contest beginning
straight away. The crowd—there were 15,000 of them present, all
in their shirt sleeves or less—cheered each man as he entered the
ring. They didn't just shout: in spite of the heat, in spite of the
sweat streaming down their walnut necks, they hauled themselves
up to bellow their plaudits while the boxers held their gloves above
their heads and bowed to left and right. At every corner of the ring
the soldiers stood in their brilliant uniforms to keep order. No one
was going to trust to mere police.

There was a long fussing about the preliminaries, but at last the
referee called the two men together into the centre of the ring.
'This is a forty-five round contest for the championship of the world.
Shake hands and come out fighting.'

The crowd were silent as the men sparred and feinted, aimed
tentative blows, and ducked out of range. Somehow Johnson's confident leer annoyed them. This was a fight, not a theatre show, wasn't
it? Halfway through the round Johnson feinted and brought over a
sumptuous left that broke like a bombshell on Willard's jaw. The
big cowboy staggered back on the ropes. There were no cheers
from the ringside seats. You saw the cigar smoke motionless in the
burning mid-day—nobody broke it by throwing his hands up and
shouting *Olé*.

The second round was featureless enough, but in the third Johnson hauled off, drew his man's guard with a right flourished at the
point, and flung home a heavy left swing to the mark. Willard's
face was thin and drawn: he was the embodiment of nervousness.
As Johnson pushed him away when he tried to clinch he beamed at
him and began to chatter. 'That's the way to do it, isn't it?' he

148

asked solicitously. 'I devoutly hope I didn't happen to hurt you, Jess.'

There wasn't much to see, so far. Only Johnson circling his man, drawing his guard to shoot home a straight left that somehow reached the giant's jaw. Only Johnson playing at will in the last half-minute of each round on point and mark, while Willard stumbled round the ring where the storm of punches drove him. In the fourth round, while bleeding from the mouth, however, Willard landed heavily on Johnson's nose.

By the fifth round you could see the fight was swinging Johnson's way. You could see, too, that the crowd didn't like it. Whenever the giant cowboy landed a tap, they got up and hollered. When Johnson bundled his man into the ropes (as he did in the fifth) and battered him at will, they jeered and booed. It wasn't any good laughing at them, or mauling Willard around as he kept up a running chatter of abuse. He didn't feel strong enough somehow—perhaps it was the sun. Anyhow, by the round's end, Willard was staggering on legs that were bent at the knee. Perhaps a couple of those famous right uppercuts would end the fight, there and then. But somehow he didn't seem to have the strength to discover those death-strokes within him. Willard still reeled, and he still landed his punches— but the fight went on.

It was all Jack's fight, of course. If there was any points decision to be given, surely he must win, in spite of the booing crowd. But in the ninth round the shape of the battle changed.

Big Willard was lazy, and slow. All his life he was to be a sluggish boxer, whom you couldn't get to face a pushover except with the referee urging him on—or as good. But even in big Willard's brain there was a sort of little down-to-earth wish to wake up after a morning nap and find himself heavyweight champion of the world. So far, big Willard had been on the receiving end, but nothing had happened.

Slowly it had dawned on the biggest and slowest man in the top bracket that you could lead to Jack Johnson and not get your tripes cut out. He had been hit, yes, but with the flap of a glove like a pillow. When he went in, whaling away with both fists, Johnson didn't step aside and pick him off—as some of them had said he would. He gave ground, and you could see the sweat breaking out on his bronze forehead.

Moreover, something else rather nice happened. When he got in close and gave Johnson a whole rattle of artillery over the ribs, the crowd got to its toes and shouted, 'Kill the black bear!' At the end of the round, Johnson, still grinning like a jackal, danced away and planted three right jabs to the ribs that blossomed with pain like the green bay tree. How the crowd howled—almost as much as he felt like howling himself.

At the end of the ninth there was a whiff of hope in Havana that big Jess might be fighting back from the floor of the ring. He'd hardly won a round yet, but he wasn't quite beaten all the same. He was faint but pursuing. There were hopes that that fine flash of aggression in the ninth meant that he was all out for victory—and he had still thirty-six rounds to get there. But the tenth round didn't suggest he was blazing a trail. The experts at the ringside remarked that they hadn't seen redder ribs in a championship contest since Jim Jeffries' hour struck.

Willard boxed on. He was tired. He wasn't just on the retreat. He was on the stumble. He reeled around under body punishment. He bent under the battery of Johnson's punches and folded up as the laughing Negro closed in on him. Johnson bent him over with big slaps that sent him rolling across the ring and wishing his footwork was quick enough to carry him out of range.

The real change came during the sixteenth round. Until then, Willard had been in the fight. Not, it is true, in the front rank of the fight, but still there—still hoping for a slip, a failure, a chance to spring in and turn the tide of battle. But the sixteenth round was embellished with a blow that had all the look of what Hazlitt called a 'settler'. Johnson landed that annihilating uppercut early on and from that moment Willard was a helpless automaton in the face of a rain of blows that shook him from stem to stern and made the customers reach for their hats. He was a beaten man, if ever you saw one: the blood-brother of Burns at Sydney, of Jeffries at Reno. It couldn't last more than a couple of rounds now.

Only . . . only here and there at the ringside there were those who wondered. Jack Johnson was thirty-seven years old. He'd fought less than half-a-dozen fights of major significance since he'd beaten Burns. He was an old man, striving to survive in a young man's game. When the bell went at the end of the twentieth round he was a mile ahead on points. If only this had been Paris—if only there had been a decision to be totted up in the referee's note-book. But it wasn't Paris; it wasn't a twenty-round fight; there wasn't a referee's decision coming. . . .

The bell rang for the twenty-first round.

The fight had slowed down now. It was a jog-trot marathon, not a gallop. The two men were both bleeding from nose and mouth, both moving sluggishly. Neither, it must be admitted, was seriously injured; and so far the fight was all Johnson's.

But in the twenty-second round the fight swung, as fights have had a way of doing since Figg beat game Ned Sutton of Gravesend. Jack Johnson went out of his corner apparently as strong as ever but the left he led to Willard was feebler than Willard had had bounced off his chin for a number of rounds, and the smile was more lackadaisical than he had seen on Johnson's mocking face since the beginning of the fight.

The steam had gone out of Jack Johnson! The fire had vanished from his punching. Instead of a black panther, licking its horrible maw for the kill, there was a weary old Negro, circling the ring with a hope of leering and grinning his way to victory. Willard sprang forward and looped out a giant's left lead to the chin. It landed. . . .

All through the twenty-second round the counter-attack poured in. The weary white forearm somehow found strength to level punches at the sagging bronze jaw. All through the round the Negro backed away and the mighty attack made him wilt as he went stiff-legged round the ring in the full gale of the assault.

The fight had turned. The battle continued to swing against the champion of the world. It was all Willard now. It was true there were two weary men in the ring, bent at the knees, their eyes glazing. But the man who led, the man who drove his victim round the ring was the white man. The stream of insults which had withered Burns and devitalized Jeffries dried up on the black lips now. There wasn't a bitter jest left to spit out. There wasn't a sneer he had strength to mutter. The rounds wore on—and they were all Willard's.

During the twenty-fifth round something happened that was to be debated as long as the Long Count of Chicago or Louis's first-round knockout of Max Schmeling. Lucille was at the ringside; and Jack sent a message to her which sent her away. There were many explanations of this act: among others the suggestion that the champion knew his hour was about to strike and was anxious that the woman he loved should not witness his eclipse. There was, of course, another version, widely accepted at the time: Johnson had sold the fight and didn't want his wife to witness his forthcoming humiliation.

The bell rang for the twenty-sixth round—the bell tolled for Johnson. He came out of his corner a tired man. The crowd around the ropes at Oriental Park and the thousands on the hills overlooking the ring may well have sensed that the end was near. That shuffling figure, with his long arms drooping and bronze shoulders sagging, was the man who years ago on just such another sunlit afternoon had clubbed Burns to defeat. This was the man who in the teeth—and the bared teeth—of the white world had battered down Jeffries and stood laughing at the world's fury as they carried his adversary out of the ring to his dressing-room.

And now it was his turn. He came forward to meet his doom.

Willard led with his left, backed away, measured his man. Then a right uppercut, swift and terrible as a blow from a cleaver, caught Johnson on the point, and the Negro bent at the knees and slid to the floor. He lay on his back, at the edge of the ring, almost through the ropes. As referee Welch shouted the count over him, he raised his glove to shade his eyes from the glare of the sun.

A fateful deed. Ever since that sun-baked afternoon that action and its implications have been argued about. Remember that Jack had sent his second to his wife; she leaves the ringside. On top of that he rolls over at the very next punch he takes—and is so far from out to the world that he shields his eyes from the sun as the count is tolled over him. . . . As soon as the rioting and pandemonium had died down—the boos for Johnson and the cheers for the new champion—the argument began. True, as they left the ring (the soldiers clearing a path for the Negro to his dressing-room), Johnson admitted that a better and younger man had beaten him fairly and squarely. True, that wonderful final punch was good enough to have knocked out any boxer in the world (and what an irony it was that it should have been a right uppercut, Johnson's own favourite blow!) but the general belief was that there was something suspicious about the end of the fight, and it is a belief that at one time Johnson himself did all he could to foster.

As late as the mid-thirties he was explaining in print to anyone who would buy the story that Jack Curley had paid him to lie down to Willard. In a statement he issued to the press he stated that the plan was that he was to go down for the count at any time between the tenth and the twentieth rounds when it appeared that Willard was boxing well enough to make such a finale plausible. As, in his opinion, Willard was never doing well enough, he had carried the fight further before throwing it away with an air of verisimilitude.

According to Johnson he had two good reasons for losing. The first was that he wanted the $50,000 he claimed Curley was prepared to pay him to lose the fight. But the second and far more important reason was that he had been assured that if he lost the fight the United States Government would consider him a person of no importance and drop the Mann Act charges pinned against him three years earlier. He would be free—so he said he had been given to believe—to return to the States, to his home, to his mother. Johnson vowed that for him losing the fight meant a bigger prize than winning it. Returning to see his mother was the ambition of his life. He was (he declared after defeat) happy to lose and would have been unhappy to win if victory meant continued exile. When he found out that defeat (as well as victory) meant continued exile, he assured the world that he had been double-crossed and that his indignation knew no bounds.

It must be noted that Jack Curley and his associate, Frazee, the theatrical producer, at once repudiated Johnson's story. They denied that they had ever assured Johnson that his prison sentence would be wiped off the records if he promised to present himself as a returning penitent who had lost his claims to glory.

Of course the possibility of such an act of benevolence had been discussed, and of course Jack Curley, like a good friend, had done all he could to enlist political help to make it possible for Johnson to return home with the assurance that his past misdeeds would be overlooked. But it is equally certain that Curley had failed, and that Johnson knew that he had failed. There was no hope of his past being forgotten if he presented himself at the frontier post—he would get no remission of his unserved sentence for having lost the Willard fight.

Thus the verdict of history refuses to accept Johnson's confession that he 'threw' the fight, and considers that he was defeated on his merits. It must not be forgotten that the precious affidavit which broke the story of the alleged cross was made just before Johnson at last entered prison, when he was in serious financial difficulties—the result, as he insisted, of his association with Jack Curley.

To-day, Nat Fleischer, the celebrated American boxing writer, owns the original of the affidavit, and heads the school of thought that refuses to believe that Johnson was beaten for any other reasons except that he was in poor physical condition and found himself up against a better man. As he said himself, while General Menocal, President of Cuba, ordered the cavalry to clear the rioting mob so that the boxers might escape to their hotels: '*I have no excuses to offer. A better and younger man has taken the championship title. . . .*'

All reigns must come to an end sooner or later. Jack Johnson's had
lasted for seven years, longer than that of any predecessor on the roll
of heavyweight title holders since the bad old days of the prize ring.
The white world had not forgotten nor forgiven him. Though
Europe was convulsed in a death-struggle, the victory of Willard at
Havana lit up many war-weary faces when the news was read in the
papers of Tuesday, 6 April 1915 that John Arthur Johnson was no
longer champion of the world.

XVI

◆◆◆

THE WILLARD FIGHT left Johnson bitter and anxious. His hopes that he could return home had been dashed; his belief that he still had a few more years at the top of his form had been pitifully exposed. There seemed no good reason for him to remain on the American continent. On the whole the best chance of earning a living and enjoying himself seemed to be in a return to Europe. In consequence, he spent the later war years in Spain, running a café in Madrid, beating two or three minor pugilists, taking part in counterspying activities for his country, and earning a little extra fame as a bull fighter.

The Spanish way of life pleased him. *Mañana sera otro dia* was as good a motto as he knew. He liked the sunshine, the complete freedom his personality basked in as a result of the absence of a colour bar. He grew fat and contented, but the news that the United States had declared war on Germany startled him out of his peaceful rut. He was eager to play his part, and hoped that at this time of crisis the past would be forgotten and he would be allowed to return to his country to enlist in the army. He soon learned that nothing was forgiven or forgotten, and that if he returned to the States he would at once be arrested to serve the sentence passed on him in his absence in 1913.

There was one thing left which he could do. He called at the American Embassy in Madrid to ask to be employed in any way which would help his country's war effort. Major Lang of the Military Attaché's office greeted him cordially. There *was* work, and it was work that should prove ideal for Johnson, if he still packed a punch. The job was in Intelligence and it consisted of helping to stop German submarine crews from putting in on the Spanish coast to take on cargoes of supplies and agents with information gained in the great open market of Madrid.

Now and then there was some agreeable strong-arm stuff, as for instance when Jack was one of a party who tracked down a seaman, apparently more Danish than Hamlet, from the café in Madrid to the submarine's lair on the Mediterranean coast. The Dane turned out to be a U-boat commander, and his crew were ready to fight it

out with knives and revolvers before Major Lang's party handed
them over to the police for abuse of neutrality. Jack himself enjoyed
his hardest bout since the Ketchel contest when engaging three of
the enemy, all of whom he managed to knock out. His hardest fight
was with the captain himself, who trespassed on Jack's old ring
technique by swearing volubly in German while trying to ram a jack-
knife into his opponent's ribs. In the end Jack stretched him out
with a rabbit-punch. He used to boast that this was the only time in
his life that he had employed this banned method of attack, which
in the unique circumstances he decided was permissible.

But the highlight of Jack's life in Spain was, of course, his initia-
tion into the bull-ring. As soon as he arrived in the country he had
made it his business to visit the bull-ring, and in a very short time
he was explaining to everyone within earshot that there was, in his
opinion, nothing unsporting about bull-fighting. It wasn't very
long before he became firm friends with some of the greatest men in
the business, including two of the most wonderful masters of the day,
Belmonte and Joselito. It was, indeed, after watching Belmonte at
work that Jack declared to Gus Rhodes that bull-fighting was the
greatest sport in the world. He also added that he wished he had
taken the easy road and given his life to this sport.

'So you think bull-fighting might be easier than boxing, Jack?'

Little Belmonte, five foot six and pale as a sheet, smiled at him
across the café table in Barcelona.

'There's more of a bull to hit,' suggested Jack.

'There's more of a bull to hit you,' remarked the magnificent
Joselito. 'Believe me, I've done both and I know which I'd prefer
any day of the week.'

The two greatest masters of their time seemed to be in conspiracy.
They had taken Jack to the bull-ring that afternoon and encouraged
the old fighter to run down the performance of a perfectly adequate
matador. It had not been difficult to do. Soon enough Johnson was
explaining to everyone within earshot what was wrong with the
matador's style and how he could be taught to improve it.

'He stands too open, my dear friends. He's asking for punishment.'

Joselito flung back his glorious head and laughed delightedly.
'Quite right,' he crowed. 'Remind me to tell Ramon. He should
cover up like the Dixie Kid, so that the bull's punches bounce off
him for twenty rounds.' He pulled at his thin black cigar. 'Why,
my poor Jack, the public would boo him out of the ring unless he

attacked all the time. And as for standing open, *I* stand open.'

'I know you do. You fight like a daredevil. One day they'll kill you. I've often wanted to tell you.'

But Joselito only laughed more uproariously than ever. For all his six feet and boxer's sturdy torso, he played around a Miuri bull as certainly and as effectively as a *maître de ballet* plays around a ballerina until the exquisite chord of destiny tells him to close to the climax. Joselito's death on the horns of a bull was still far distant, on the other side of many a golden and triumphal afternoon.

'If I were a bull-fighter I wouldn't risk myself the way you do,' Jack told him. 'I'd make the public think I was within inches of death, but I'd keep my margin of safety *always*. I did in the ring. My God, against the men I beat when I was at my best, I was padding backwards round the ring for three rounds out of four. Defence *always* wins fights in the end, if it's good enough. Why, I beat some of the best men I ever fought by making them lead to me, and then smashing home on the biceps as their punches came up at me. I had old Jeffries wincing with pain that way before I ever hit him on the jaw.'

Belmonte looked thoughtful. He sipped his *rioja* and stared at Jack as if he was trying to believe what he heard. 'But José's right. The crowd want you to carry the fight forward in the bull-ring all the time. You must make the bull show all his powers of attack, and reveal that you're a split second ahead of him all the time. You're partners in a dance, but you're the master. Only when you've shown that you're in command must you bring the dance to an end. And then in a dazzling flicker of an instant! The sword must flash too quickly for the eye to follow it. The bull drops helpless before you, like the woman at the dance's end.'

'That's bull-fighting,' said Joselito. 'The killing of the bull is the poem we write to the woman we love. The poem must have all the bells of heaven chiming in it.'

Little Belmonte waved at the crowd passing down the Ramblas; the women casting languishing looks at him, every young stranger of spirit waving jauntily in the hope of a nod. 'A greater glory than fighting, Jack. When you fight a man there are rules, and there is no death. Nothing but a sham fight, my friend! A battle of roses.'

Jack shrugged his shoulders. 'I'm not denying yours is about the greatest sport in the world. I've already admitted it.'

'Sport, Jack—it's not sport. It's art and poetry, and the most wonderful climax a love-affair can have. If you were a woman—

which would you rather, have a great Murube bull dedicated to you, or sleep with a Prince?'

Joselito's eyes were dreamy with pride, but Belmonte continued to watch Jack as calculatingly as a pawnbroker.

'You'll find it's as good as that, Jack. Especially the first time.'

The boxer stared. True, he had spent the best part of the afternoon explaining in detail the technique of the successful bullfighter. But that didn't mean that he knew anything at all about it. 'Well, wait a moment. I'm—well, I'm over thirty, you know. That's no time to start a career as a matador.'

'You're thirty-eight, Jack. You must take the chance *now*, while you're still young enough. In a year or two's time you'll be too slow, and your concentration will have gone.'

'Yes, but look here, the thing's a ritual. I don't even know the rules. I'd offend against all the gods of the game.'

'You needn't worry, José and I will teach you. We wouldn't dare let you appear looking like a novice—a protégé of ours. They'd spit at us, the next time we came into the ring.'

'You're not afraid, Jack, by any chance?' Joselito asked innocently. 'Because if you are, that's an end of it, of course. The bullring's no place for any man with fear in his heart.'

Jack Johnson sprang up so that the glasses rattled on the little table. 'I'm your man, my friends. What Spanish hidalgos can do, a Negro from Texas can manage. Name your day and pick your bull —and lead me to him.'

Joselito wrung the podgy black hand. 'That's a hundred pesetas you owe me,' he said to Belmonte. 'I told you he'd be a sucker.'

It was a Sunday in July, hot enough for Texas, when Jack made his first appearance as a matador in the bull-ring in Barcelona. Joselito and Belmonte had been as good as their word. They had not failed him. He wore the golden-striped satin trousers Joselito had worn when all but gored in the hardest battle of his life in Valencia. He carried a cloak that a champion of the past had flourished like a flag of victory. And Belmonte's sword, beautiful and inevitable as the final couplet of a sonnet, graced his side.

As soon as he was dressed, Belmonte took him by the arm. 'Now for the chapel. I will teach you the prayer all matadors have said since the history of bulls began.'

Jack shrugged his shoulders. He was a Catholic and frightened of the unknown as any ex-champion of the world could be, but his arrogance was strong. 'Not for me, this afternoon. You go and pray for the bull.'

Belmonte's eyes narrowed. 'You will pray all the same, my friend. When you are on your knees you will find that faith dies hard—harder than bulls.'

He caught a glimpse of the crowd at the bottom of a stairway. There were thousands of them—tens of thousands, perhaps. He stood there for a moment, straining to focus his eyes in the glare on the men and women on the far side of the arena. The women around the ringside! Glorious looking girls, with eyes that flashed demurely, or eagerly, or undressed you as you stood there before them; with smiles that beckoned or taunted. Girls whose conversation was as prim as responses in church; girls who weren't allowed to spend five minutes alone with a man in a café unless his parents had known their parents for twenty years—here they were in black mantillas at the bull-ring, eyes glittering, teeth gleaming, appetite for blood and death keen as the hunger of tigers at feeding time.

And suddenly it struck him that it might be *his* death that would satisfy their appetites. He had beaten boxers by getting inside their skins, figuring out what they would try to do against Jack Johnson, and being one step ahead of them each time. But what did he know about the mind of a bull? How to get inside a bull's brain and guess the way it worked out a fight? He remembered all the things bull-fighters had ever told him. *You never get two of them alike.* And— *you might as well call them foxes; when they're dead on their feet they throw in the fastest, hardest charge of the day.* And one of them had said: *All the gifts you must have—speed, youth, fearlessness. But they are as nothing compared with experience.*

It suddenly struck him that he had none of the qualifications a matador must possess. He was yards slower than he had been at his best; he was old, as fighters went. When you battled for your life, eight years past thirty wasn't eight years: it was a whole generation past your prime. And he wasn't fearless. You were only fearless when you were young, brilliant and stupid. Last night he'd dreamed of his funeral; the long line of flower-laden cars; Lucille blubbering into the collar of her new sable coat. Gus Rhodes talking to press-men who'd quote him as saying: *He was the whitest black man in boxing's history.*

But again and again, he came back to his inexperience. You had to learn bull-fighting, from the beginning, with death at stake. He wished he had watched the champions in the past more closely, instead of just observing their mistakes so that he could turn them to good account in conversation.

Then, suddenly, he saw the women spring up across the arena; he heard the shriek of the crowd; the scream of terror that turned into volleying cheers of acclamation. And in that instant fears and doubts left him. He was alone now in his naked pride of power. Battle was his province. Who challenged him, he would fight to the death. He was Jack Johnson, the peerless Johnson, lusting in the glory of the kill, dedicating to the woman he loved the body of the vanquished.

Belmonte touched his arm. 'The President has gone to your dressing-room,' he said. 'He is paying you the great honour of calling upon you before you go into the ring.'

The President stood talking to Joselito, and he dwarfed the great bull-fighter. He had a face like a mountain crag, bony and bleak and untouched by the sun. He gave Jack Johnson the bow a grandee might offer to a famous foreigner. 'You are a brave man, Mr Johnson. You are not content to have been a champion of the world. After your career is over, you risk everything for the first time.'

Jack smiled, hoping the words were meant as a frigid jest. 'When I saw Belmonte for the first time, I knew that I had given my life to the wrong trade. This was the most beautiful and exacting sport in the world.'

The President bowed on behalf of all the bulls in Spain. 'You will allow me to give you one piece of advice.'

One more infallible rule! Well, what did one more matter? He had digested an encyclopædia on the subject from all the *afficionados* ever since it was announced he was to appear in a ring.

'If you want to survive, Mr Johnson—and I hope you will—you must *never* take your eyes off the bull. Not for one second. Not for one tenth part of one second. There is no minute's rest between rounds in bull-fighting.'

Again the grandee's stiff little bow. Again the piercing glance from under the craggy eyebrows. They all stood back in silence, and the President passed from the room.

'Your turn next, Jack,' said José. 'How did you get on in the draw?'

Belmonte gave his sad little smile. 'He had his usual luck. He drew the smallest bull in the history of Barcelona. A bull about the size of a cat.'

'Tough luck, Jack. They say the bigger the bull, the louder the cheer. Never mind, you're a curiosity. The crowd will probably grant you the bull's tail out of good manners to a stranger.'

'Always supposing that the smallest bull in history doesn't get Jack's tail,' suggested Belmonte.

There was a stir in the corridor, a roar from the sunlit world of the far-away arena. A little man with the brown stub of a cigarette peeping out from his moustache bounced into the room and bowed to Jack as if he had been a prince. The hour had struck.

He was alone at last. He walked up the long dark corridor so many had taken before him: boys from little mountain villages whose parents had prayed for that day as other parents pray for the day of their son's ordination; carefree heroes who found it hard to wait till the victory was won, and evening brought more brilliant glances of admiration and more passionate kisses—the long, dark corridor down which they had carried away many a hero whose mind had wavered from his work, whose proud parents were still on their knees.

Then—suddenly—sunlight! Blazing light like the sunshine of the deep South, the dazzling light in which the world shimmers and will not settle down. The crowd were on their feet now. There were women clapping their white hands above their heads, tearing the scarlet roses from their black hair, hurling them down at the tiny figure in the arena below—women blowing him kisses from their exquisite, scented finger-tips. With his hand on the hilt of the sword, he bowed to them, and to the President in his box. With a gesture he dedicated his bull to the old grandee, who rose to bow to him.

And now the thrill of the great occasion possessed him like a passion, so that he felt almost dizzy as the cheers rolled round the amphitheatre, flashing like a rainbow of gleaming colours in the torrential midsummer sunlight. The thrill passed, the dazed moment was gone. He became, in an instant, a fighter again—a fighter concentrating on the hardest job of a lifetime.

Across the ring—the bull! The bull that was to be the size of a cat. The smallest bull in the history of Barcelona. . . . He was a monster! He was big and black as a steam engine, and as heavy in the chest. As he gazed on him, Jack guessed what had happened. Juan, the big matador from Seville, with a mouth like a snarling dog's, had bribed the men in charge to switch bulls. Juan himself had killed the bull as small as a cat, and left his own bull, the outsize monster of the day, for Jack to deal with. For Juan could not forgive Jack his presence in the bull-ring at all. 'He has no right here,' he had said in Belmonte's presence. 'He has served no apprenticeship as I had to serve it. Let him keep to the boxing ring, if he isn't too old and too fat to fight. We won't intrude on him there.' And when Belmonte had attempted to soothe him, Juan had snarled like a dog with hydrophobia: 'You tell him to keep away. If he goes into the ring, it won't be only the bull who'll be against him.'

And now Juan had worked his trick. For all the work *banderilleros* and *picadores* had put into the fight, this huge bull was still strong as ever, only now roused to his full ferocity. As the beast pawed the ring, churning it to red dust beneath his hoof, Jack found himself thinking that the odds were against the matador. He began what was in fact the last round of the fight—cold: but the bull was worked up to the transports and ecstasies of conflict.

And here he came! The other side of the bull-ring seemed a world away—he would never arrive. Oh, for the little ring where he had fought Burns, where there hadn't been room to withdraw like an army, and come back into the campaign with the distant thunder of a cavalry charge! The distant thunder. . . . Time stood still. . . . Then, before you were ready, before you could brace yourself—he was on you. Jack had just time to flourish the *muleta* and sidestep, and the bull was thundering by with a whistling snort as he chucked his head into the air. The first brush of the final round was over, and as Jack spun round on his heel, his strained face broke into a gleaming smile. This was easy! The big chap was slow—slower than Jeffries. You could wait longer, electrifying the crowd with your brilliant daring, and never really take a risk at all. Then he told himself to beware. This was only the first charge. Perhaps now he had got to close-quarters the bull would have more cunning, more speed in attack.

Here he came again—and again Jack slid away from him with time in hand. But the third charge was a different thing altogether. Jack hadn't the time to sidestep like a ballet dancer as he plunged in. The space covered by the sweep of the dagger-sharp horns gave him no room to manœuvre. He swerved away somehow and felt a pang of pain across his thigh. His trouser-leg was ripped; the bull's near horn had gashed him. Had he been a fraction of a second slower the beast would have dug his vitals out.

No more tricks or risks—he must knock out his challenger at the first chance now! As the bull turned towards him, he found himself wishing he was stripped to the waist; this uniform of the matador seemed to weigh him down, to restrict every swift movement he must make for survival. He felt the heat too; the stifling, windless sunshine in which a man could only give of his best when stripped to his glowing skin for action.

And now the bull was upon him again, a tensed, compact black engine of destruction, the darts quivering in the hunched bulk of his deeply-muscled shoulders. He tried the pose Belmonte had shown him: *the mill*, with the *muleta* rippling round his legs as the beast swung by. He heard the crowd crow—he knew that they were greeting his tyro's efforts with laughter as well as cheers.

But it was no laughing matter to him. He felt himself growing tired; he knew that in this phase of a fight concentration would flicker, and he remembered again the President's words: '*Never take your eyes off the bull. Not for one second. Not for one tenth part of one second.*'

A pity a bull couldn't understand English! If only he could have taunted him as he had taunted Tommy and big Jim. . . . 'You're yellow . . . you can't take it. Come on in, if you dare, only you don't dare. You've got the guts of a louse, white trash, you big mouth-fighter. . . .' He found himself shouting taunts at the bull, and grinning at him to show he despised him and was playing with him. He remembered all Belmonte had told him about the death stroke. The body springing up, poised on the toes; the eyes fixed on the spot on the neck where the great black shoulders met; the hand steady and swift as an eagle in its pounce—the wrist like a steel spring. . . .

And he failed. The sword came from behind the curtain of the *muleta* fast enough, he whipped home for the fatal spot with lightning speed—but he missed. . . . He heard the roars of the crowd change to groans. He knew that the President's nose would be an inch higher than ever. He could see Juan's dog-teeth gleam in a snarl that was half a sneering laugh.

Again the charge—and again failure. All the coaching of Belmonte meant nothing when the moment of crisis was upon him. He hadn't the concentration, there wasn't the co-ordination between hand and eye. He was too old—too old and too slow. He heard the groans of the crowd, with here and there a cat-call. The sweat froze on his face. He felt his arms weighted down by his heavy uniform; he knew that the matador's hat must look ridiculous on his black poll. A panic shook him like a *frisson*: next time the bull would skewer him as he had not been able to skewer the bull.

The bull was turning, pawing the ground again, focussing him in its red, glaring eyes. The bull was spurning the ground on its last charge for death or glory. And this time he made no mistake. He rose to his toes, whirled the *muleta* as Belmonte had taught him, saw the bull's head give its murderous toss away from him, saw the spot between the shoulder blades, and plunged the long, shivering sword in to the hilt.

He saw the great railway engine halt in its tracks: the smoke from the nostrils: the red glare from the lamplight of its glazing eyes. It was stopped in its length, and heaving with the effort of keeping the flame of life yet flickering. He stared at it, fascinated. He had beaten this monster, more decisively than he had ever beaten Langford or Ketchel. It stood there before him, all hatred and power, yet convulsed in the agony of death. Then its front legs seemed to fold up under it; it sank forward slowly, and slowly it rolled on to its gored yet massive side. It was a dead bull. A child could safely kick the flank of what had been the primed engine of destruction a few minutes ago.

He heard the groans turn into cheers; the cheers swell into an unbroken roar of applause. Far away on the other side of the arena he saw the first barefoot boys clamber into the ring and make for him, waving and cheering. The crowd came flooding after. Suddenly he felt young again: young and light—the matador's uniform was light as a pair of boxing trunks. He waved his hand to the President's box. Then the crowd engulfed him, swept him up shoulder high, carried him laughing, kissing, hugging, around the arena and out to his dressing-room.

When they had barred the doors and the cheering was a distant thunder, like a storm at sea heard over a mountain-range, Belmonte flung his arm about his neck. 'Ah, but Jack, that time he slashed your thigh, I thought he had you. I was sure he had you. I prayed for you then, Jack. If that bull had known as much about bullfighting as I do, you would have been a dead matador!'

XVII

++

THE WAR WAS OVER. Perhaps it was going to be a brave new world with the black deeds of the past wiped out, like every nation's debt to America, except Finland's. Perhaps, now that he wasn't a world's champion any more and a white man ruled the roost, they'd let Jack come home again. It was queer how he yearned for home! Even in his most successful days they'd never treated him as well in Chicago as they had in Paris or Madrid. Now he wasn't champion, they'd treat him at best as just another bit of black trash, and see he didn't pollute the street-car in which a white prostitute might ride who'd be glad to sell herself to him for five dollars on Friday night. In Madrid and Paris he was a personality: a prince, if you liked. In America he might be no more than a prisoner. Yet it was to America that his dreams and aspirations turned.

Well, if his own country still spurned him, there was a neighbour who held out welcoming arms. Mexico would like to see him in the ring: the invitation was backed by no less a personage than his old enemy, President Carranza himself. Johnson accepted and went to Mexico City to fight several selected opponents, none of them very important in the history of pugilism. The best of them was Tom Cowler of England, who had been beaten by Battling Levinsky, Jack Dillon, Fred Fulton, Frank Moran, Billy Hicks, but who was a respected trial horse all the same.

They didn't, in those days, grade pugilists in order of merit but, if they had, no one would have named Tom Cowler among the world's top twenty. Nevertheless most of the citizens of Mexico City with the price of an admission ticket came to watch the fight. One can sympathize with their curiosity. If one could have had the choice of watching a bloated, ageing Jack Johnson shuffling round the ring ten years after reaching his prime or the rip-roaring Marciano at his best, not a few would prefer to waste their money on the former experience rather than invest it in the latter. *And did you once see Shelley plain* . . .

Tom Cowler was game, game as a pebble. He was on the receiving end for eleven rounds when Jack, exhausted from handing out extra rations of punishment, muttered to him: 'Why don't you give it up, Tom?'

Cowler dodged a right swing and replied humbly: 'I shall, when you leave me alone.' The end came in the following round.

Jack's other fights included matches with Paul Samson, Monte Cutler, and Captain Bob Roper. None of them gave him any serious amount of trouble and he had arranged to take part in other fights when he received the tip that, as you had to expect in Mexico, revolution was once again scheduled to break out. There was a rumble in the back streets, and brawlers under a strange flag in the poorest quarters of the city. There were inflammatory speeches under the windows of the great Cathedral and torches pitched through the jewel-bright glass and the songs of a rising people on the march. 'Obregon for President!' shouted the shoeblacks in the city square. 'Death to Carranza!' cried the factory workers choking the streets before the great white palace which the police guarded with crossed rifles and which they might point either way when the hour struck.

In the last day of his reign of power Carranza found time to warn his new friend Johnson of the coming struggle and arrange for his escape from the capital. The fast car slid through the outskirts of the city and picked up the special train that was waiting in the suburbs. Far away in the oleander-scented night you could hear the first shots fired in the final round of the struggle for power.

Johnson's train took him north to a port from which he took ship for Tia Juana. The town was quiet as an alfalfa farm, and the arrival of the great fighter woke the citizens out of their siesta. The impresarios had calculated correctly when they decided that a few contests featuring the ex-world champion would attract American tourists over the border. It was delightful to Jack to find himself idolized by his own countrymen again, after competently taking care of moderate opposition in the ring.

'If that's the way they feel about me,' he said to Lucille, 'perhaps it would be safe to go home at last.'

She shrugged her shoulders. 'They don't want revenge, Jack. It's just that you've flouted the law, and you'll have to pay.'

It was a point he seemed unable to follow objectively. Always he saw the question of his treatment on return as a personal matter: a battle between himself who had (he felt) done some service to his country, and a Government who had to be persuaded not to persecute him because of the colour of his skin.

Well, his mother was dead now, he had nothing much to lose.

For a while there flickered in him a hope that he might skip across the border without formality and take his place unnoticed in the Negro society of Chicago. It was Tom Carey, a Chicago politician, who advised him to attempt no such thing.

'You *want* to go home, Jack? You *really* want to go home?'

'I do. I've thought it over, I've found out what I can get out of life away from the States, and I want to go back. My family are there, and whatever friends I have.'

'Then go to the border, and surrender your passport. That way, you give yourself up to their mercy. The law must take its course, but why should they come down heavy on you? Take a chance on the clemency of the United States of America.'

That night he said to Lucille: 'I'm going to do it, honey. I'm going home.'

Next day he drove to the border at San Diego. A policeman sunning himself by the frontier-post said the Sheriff would be right back in a minute. Some devil of a Mexican had stolen a couple of his chickens the night before, and he had to telephone to the authorities.

A tall fresh-faced man came out of the house, buttoning up his uniform. 'I'm the Sheriff. They said you were wanting me.'

'That's right. Here's my passport. I'm wanted in Chicago, Sheriff, for breaking bail seven years ago. My name's Jack Johnson.'

The Sheriff thrust out a huge hand. 'My, my, this *is* an honour. What my boy in Santa Barb will say when he hears about this! And how have you been keeping, Jack?'

He didn't know how they'd receive him back in Chicago. Seven years ago it had seemed to him he hadn't a friend in the town. The whites wanted him dead or alive, but preferably the former. His own folk were glad to see the back of him; he was only stirring up trouble for them and bringing race riots nearer. But now Chicago was ready to welcome him home. Throughout the Negro quarter the word was passed like a secret message on drums through the jungle: 'Jack Johnson's back!'

Ten thousand Negroes crowded round the station to welcome him. The authorities weren't running any risks, however. They took him from the train at Joliet, and quickly clapped him into prison to await his trial.

It couldn't be said (on Jack's own admission) that the Law treated him harshly; either then or when it had confirmed the sentence passed on him. If he gave a true picture of his sufferings and humiliations, 'Tiny' Johnson had worried unduly about the degradation in store for her beloved son. While awaiting trial, Jack was allowed out of Joliet three nights a week, until the papers complained that he was being treated too indulgently, and he was transferred to another prison outside Chicago. Here, just to show those journalists that they weren't running the country, he was allowed to go home every night.

Nor had he anything to fear when the law pronounced its penalty. The old conviction still stood, and his sentence was confirmed at a year's imprisonment. Nothing is less precise than a sentence of imprisonment passed upon a Negro by an American court. It can mean hell upon earth, as it meant in later years to the Scottsborough Boys in various prisons of the deep South. For Johnson—again according to his own statement—it meant a life of comfort and dignity, with a standard of living few citizens outside the bars could fail to envy.

When he arrived at Leavenworth Prison, Kansas, Warden Anderson greeted him with a kindness that was, as far as Johnson was concerned, several degrees better than paternal. There was the cordial handshake, the reassuring slap on the back, the friendly words: 'Now, Jack, be a good boy and you'll be out in a few months.' Deputy Warden Fisher was as jovial and as just as Warden Anderson. Jack had never received fairer or better treatment from white men in his life.

He was allowed, before entering Leavenworth, to stop off in Kansas City for a night out. He took the opportunity to throw a party which Lucille had to admit was as good as anything she remembered in Paris or Barcelona. But the good parties did not stop outside prison. Inside, Jack was allowed his own cook, and seems to have lived comfortably indeed. There was, of course, no brutal insistence that he should actually remain behind bars all the time. He was allowed out daily, and, as a result of the regular business meetings he held with Lucille and Gus Rhodes, was able to knock up a respectable income as a fight promoter.

It must not be assumed, however, that he neglected his prison duties. He was made Director of Physical Training at Leavenworth, an appointment which gave him more satisfaction than being elected a Freemason in Scotland in 1911. The inmates should learn Joy through Strength, or his name wasn't Li'l Arthur. One can imagine the enthusiasm of many an ancient felon on learning that he was to find redemption through a brisk course of shadow-boxing, or regular attendance on the punch-bag.

But there were treats for the gang (if one may use such a phrase) as well as a new working schedule. 'Jack,' said the Warden one fine spring morning, 'why don't you make a comeback?'

Jack stared. But for Them he wouldn't have retired. His last fight at Tia Juana had been just a day or two before They had taken him in tow.

'Well, I sort of figured I'd be a bit on the old side by the time I got out of the calaboose,' he admitted.

'Why wait till you get out of the calaboose?'

He laughed. It was all very well getting time off to set himself up as promoter on the side. He could hardly hope for time off to take in a return match with Willard in New York. Besides, what about the road work? Wouldn't those nosy customers of the press want to know what it was all about if they came on Jack Johnson jogging along through the open country around Leavenworth?

'No, Jack, I don't mean a big fight under Tex Rickard. That'll have to wait. But why not a fight here, in prison? We could provide some pretty fair opposition, it seems to me.'

Why not indeed? What would make a better treat for all than a fight on Thanksgiving Day? If it came to that—why not a couple of fights? He was fitter than he'd been for years; fitter than he was when he fought Moran in Paris, fitter than when he killed his bull in Barcelona. He'd need to sharpen up with a little sparring, but there were men in Leavenworth who were good enough to act as sparring partners to anyone.

And on Thanksgiving Day, 1920, he made his come-back. The prison was decked out with flowers and bunting for the occasion, and the prison band played all his favourite tunes. It was as if a favourite son was being welcomed back to his home town. He felt a pang of nervousness as he slipped into the ring to a roar of applause. Would he deserve his ovation? He was pretty old now, as boxers went. His judgment of distance wasn't what it was, and what about his stamina? Still, as the Warden said, a guy could only do his best, and it wasn't as if he was being asked to fight Sam McVey.

His first opponent was big enough, however, to set the trusties at the ringside gobbling with excitement. They hadn't seen an outsize customer like seventeen-stone George Owen since Barnum came to town. And George, though no Jim Corbett, knew the elements of the game, and could probably have punched his way through a stone wall. Jack's footwork had to be at its best to keep George at bay, and the way the old master slid out of trouble, ducked, slipped and rode punches won admiration from men who hadn't had a chance of admiring boxing at its best since Joe Gans was in the head-lines. For several rounds Jack let his man lead to him and counter-punched handsomely. Then, in the fifth round, he stormed into attack. A quick left stabbed the air, and Owen's guard came down. The right went over dazzlingly fast; and Owen's head twisted on his neck. Jack was after him like an Aberdeen Angus bull. Another right! Up from the hip it came, beautifully aimed to find the angle of the jaw. And another—and another! Four grand rights, shaking the giant to his foundations, but not sapping them. Well—Johnson was forty-two. A man didn't punch his weight at forty-two. He was lucky to learn this stern lesson of his depreciation in the comfort and security of prison rather than in the pitiless world outside. Here there were no sour critics asking where his punch had gone to: only a crowd of old friends cheering each right swing as it went home as if it were the crack of doom.

And in the sixth round he put Owen away. For a few seconds he looked like a world-beater all over again. There was the feint, the shift, the right to the point. And there was Owen spreadeagled at his feet, as it might have been Ketchel.

He didn't leave the ring as they helped George Owen back to the inviolate safety of his cell. He stayed in his corner, waiting for the next challenger to appear, and swiftly ran over his form in his mind's eye. He hadn't, of course, the speed or the punch; but in one respect he felt that his warmest admirer would have been proud of his showing against Owen. He had fought the giant with his fists—never with his tongue. A clean, gentlemanly fighter, this Jack Johnson! Well, when Owen pushed his way between the ropes he had dedicated him to Warden Anderson as he had dedicated the big boys on the Pacific Coast to Sadie, and as he had dedicated his bull to the President of the Barcelona bull-ring. He couldn't let Warden Anderson down by any display of conduct unworthy of a Leaven-worth man.

And here came Topeka Jack Johnson, his opponent in the second contest. Topeka was an old sparring partner of his, and he knew every trick the fellow kept in the bag. It was more an exhibition bout than a match, but he was a jump ahead all the time and an easy winner at the end of the bout.

Two victories in one day! Not bad for an old 'un—come to think of it, he hadn't tackled such a programme since he'd fought in Battle Royals as a kid in Galveston. The Governor shook him by the hand. The crowd cheered him louder than the crowd had cheered in Sydney: he found himself looking back down the long corridor of the years and wondering what had happened to the Negro kid who'd fallen off the fence as he ducked in imitation of himself when Burns had telegraphed that big right in the twelfth round. A thin black hand was laid on his glove. He came back from Sydney, from Boxing Day 1908, to bend down to a tiny old man serving the last years of his life-sentence. 'Well done, Jack—well done, indeed. This makes you Heavyweight Champion of Leavenworth Prison.'

It was as handsome a compliment as he had been paid in years.

The months sped by, and Warden Anderson was as good as his word. He sent a fine report to headquarters and on his recommendation a parole came for Johnson with three months of his sentence still to run. He was not allowed, however, to slip out into the great world unnoticed. The Warden gave him a farewell worthy of the occasion: a thousand prisoners were assembled to whom Johnson delivered a valedictory address in a highly moral vein. He pulled out every stop and there were not many dry eyes in his audience.

And that was that. The gates were open at last: he could return to the world as a free man. Only—free to do what? His great days as a fighter were over. If he could draw a crowd anywhere outside prison it must be as a freak, a fragment of the historic past. He could scrape up a little money perhaps by promoting minor fights, and exhibiting himself in the ring before the customers. But there wasn't much of a living to be earned in that way; the big money to be made out of the fight game was becoming increasingly concentrated in the hands of the very few men at the top. He couldn't compete with Rickard. He was still a Negro, even though he had served his prison sentence.

For a year or two he hung around the outskirts of the boxing world. Indeed it wasn't till 1924 that he appeared in the ring for the last time. Then he beat Homer Smith in ten rounds in Montreal, but he gave a miserable exhibition in winning his final fight.

Of course, he wasn't a rich man. He had been broke when he raised the dough to bury Sam McVey, and that term of imprisonment can have added little to his capital. Nothing is grimmer than the future of an ex-champion who has lost his fortune. The restaurant with his name over the door passes into other hands: it may still bear his name, but he won't be invited to sit down to a plate of Irish stew in it. He can see a picture of himself at the wheel of his car in the advertisement columns of the newspapers, but the car has long ago been sold and he now has to count the money in his pocket before he takes his place in the bus queue. The sort of job he is offered comes from men he instinctively distrusts; and when pay day comes around he worries as to whether he is going to be short-changed. Perhaps like Louis, he will attempt to escape poverty by a return to the ring, facing, long out of season, punch-drunkenness and double vision rather than the pennilessness that Sam Langford knew, or the return to the gutter that was the fate of the great Griffo. Only the best behaved and best bred may, like Benny Leonard, be welcomed back to the game as third man in the ring, after they have ceased to be first man in it.

It was a blank future Jack Johnson had to face, after his retirement in 1924. Moreover he was to have to earn himself a living for another twenty-two years of virtual inactivity.

XVIII

++

THE SISTER AT ST. AGNES HOSPITAL, Raleigh, North Carolina, pulled the curtains round the bed. There hadn't been a hope, From the moment they'd brought him in, she'd known he hadn't any chance.

The smash had come twenty miles north of Raleigh on Highway Number One. The patient (she still thought of them as patients until their bodies were removed to the morgue) had been driving a big car which had skidded off the road and hit an electric light pole. The car had overturned, and the driver had been shockingly injured. His passenger (his name was Fred L. Scott) was slightly hurt. Some people had all the luck.

The ward doctor opened the door. The screens told him what he wanted to know.

'Just now?' he asked.

'Two minutes ago.'

He went back to his office and wrote on a form: 6.10 *p.m.*, *June* 10, 1946. *Patient's Name–John Johnson. Cause of Death–Multiple injuries from car accident.*

Somebody tapped on his door. 'Come!' he said irritably. He hated people to tap: he was there whenever anybody wanted him. The intern who came in looked as if he had been seeing visions. 'Gosh, Jim, do you know who that was?'

There was a case down at the bottom of the ward the doctor wanted to see: an old man who'd been run into, but who still had a chance. His mind was on him and he wasn't listening. 'I don't know who he is. Come to that, I don't know what you're talking about.'

'The accident case. The guy who just died.'

The doctor looked down at his pad. 'Johnson,' he said. 'Not Samuel Johnson, just John.'

The intern didn't laugh. 'Crissake,' he said. 'It's true then. Jim —that's him. That's Jack Johnson.'

The doctor got slowly to his feet. He walked into the ward, leaving the door open behind him for the first time in his life. Ever since he was a kid, there'd been just one hero he'd wanted to see. Now he was going to fulfil his ambition.

The last twenty-two years had been the happiest of Jack's life, and the least eventful. He'd turned his hand to a lot of things. He'd peddled whisky; led an orchestra, opened a gym in New York, trained boxers, worked in a saloon; carried a spear in *Aïda* as an Ethiopian general wearing a leopard-skin ('the job is yours as long as you promise not to sing'); and been a cabaret entertainer. When he had a few bucks in hand he announced to the press that he was re-writing *Othello*, when he could spare the time from listening to concerts. 'All music affects me deeply,' he had told them, 'I love opera especially. All Wagner. Puccini too. And *Faust*—one of my favourite works of art.'

Then he would tell the boys if they could be persuaded to stick around and listen that reading was just as important to him as listening to music. He liked to curl up with Gibbon's *Decline and Fall* just as much as he had liked to read Herbert Spencer in his younger days. And he was a real student of biography too, come to think of it. He'd read every biography of Napoleon he could lay his hands on.

Then there was the time when he turned evangelist. Let it not be hinted for a moment that his faith was other than sincere and consuming in intensity. All the same it wasn't everybody's faith. As he explained it to those interested in his conversion, he hadn't seen the light of Christianity only. He'd added to it all the illumination he had found in Buddhism and Confucianism. For some reason his evangelism hadn't caught on: people hadn't really got serious minds after World War I.

It was in 1937 that he first got himself engaged to lecture at Hubert's Museum at 228 West 42nd Street. He got up before an audience once a year or oftener and told them all about his 109 fights, so many of which he had won by knock-outs. If the audience was warm he might be tempted to slip in Willard's tribute to him, paid not so long ago. 'Jack Johnson,' he had observed. 'Why, on the form he showed at thirty-seven when I fought him, he could have handled Joe Louis and Billy Conn simultaneously.' Those lectures at the Museum went pretty well, all things considered, though it was a bit annoying when the gossips insisted that what Jack Johnson had sunk to was acting as bouncer for a flea circus. Not that he wasn't perfectly capable of doing the job, if there happened to be a staff crisis.

It was a satisfaction to Jack that these lectures were a success. They gave him an opening for a wider life. Why shouldn't he go round the country giving personal appearances at fêtes and fairs everywhere? At Hubert's the public paid ten cents to hear him, and for the money the customers got a chance of listening to the truth about the greatest fights of his career and of asking questions which were always courteously and carefully answered. The crowd liked the show so much that Jack had to give several performances in the course of a working day. He certainly dragged the customers away from Hubert's other attractions: the flea circus, the fruit machines, the dancing show and the rifle range.

Those who chose Johnson saw a well-dressed, quiet-spoken man with face unmarked after some twenty years in the ring, who looked ten years younger than his age. It was known that he was happily married to the wife who was to survive him, and he was quick to declare that he had 'found God and was quite content with his lot in life, harbouring a grudge against no man'.

Though his wealth was gone with the wind, he was in constant work when he extended his activities beyond New York and certainedly earned $40 a week, and possibly more. He had the reputation of being a generous man; his old suspicion of his fellow mortals seemed to have vanished with the mellowing years. He had an apartment in Chicago, and was trying to find one in New York.

He had developed a curious streak of modesty in his old age. The well-known Cockney writer, Fred Bason, who has collected the autographs of most of the famous from George Washington to G.B.S., persuaded a friend to ask Johnson for his signature at one of the lectures in Hubert's Museum. The man who was never tired of assuring the world that he was the destined saviour of the Negro race was reluctant to sign. He said, 'It gives a false sense of values for me to autograph a card.' In the end he was persuaded to write his name, but he did so with reluctance.

The star turn of the dime museums! It wasn't quite what he'd expected of life, thirty years back. He remembered the £200 that had to be scraped up to get himself and Sam Fitzpatrick over to Australia—and the fortunes that had piled up since that little trip. He chuckled as he thought of the great crowd that had hurled abuse at him on that sunny day at Reno when he'd whipped Jeffries—the white race had been so angry about that little business that they'd swiftly passed a law forbidding interstate commerce in motion pictures of boxing matches, lest the whole of America should see what a black man had done to their precious champion. He was important enough to force them to make special laws in those days—and now he was the star turn of the dime museums. . . . Oh well, it couldn't be helped. He was due to travel down to Texas to appear with a circus there. He got into the car in a mood of cheerful anticipation.

And it was a delightful visit, as he had expected. The best of it was at night when he could walk around Galveston alone. There was the beach he'd lain on, on so many blazing days of boyhood, with the town shimmering in the heat haze behind the great docks and warehouses of the waterfront. There was the place where he'd begun as a fighter, beating the daylight out of Bob Tomlinson who'd come to Galveston as the star of a circus, just as he himself had now, more than half a century later.

He looked back at the foot of the hill, at the silent sea which had sprung up like a lion and torn the town apart half a lifetime ago. There was the corner where he had last seen Ambrose, and down there the watermelon boy had been sitting when they'd pinched his cycle—he could see the expression on his face now, forty-six years after. Here was where he had fought Harry the Carter among the floods. To-night he was prouder of winning that fight than of beating any of the men whose names resounded in history.

The moon shone on the old house where 'Tiny' Johnson had belted him for losing a fight at school. It hadn't changed—he could have sworn that cracked window-pane on the first floor had been there when he and his brother Charley slept in that room. The boys playing in the alley down the road might have been the kids in his gang.

Well, it was good to be back, to see again one or two old-timers who said they'd known him before ever he put his fist into a boxing glove: they might have been telling the truth, at that. In return he made an effort to tell them the best story he knew when he gave his lecture that night. He made Fitzsimmons live again for them: they could see the bald brow with its fringe of red whisker, the barrel-chest, the spindly legs and pipe-stem arms. They could hear his terrific punches sing across the ring. They could see Gentleman Jim Corbett, the prettiest boxer ever, as Jack had first seen him at the Opera House in Chicago in white silk tights and black stockings, sparring with Steve O'Donnell. They could see himself as a young fighter in Chicago. Nobody wanted him—'the woods are full of fighters' they had told him. But somehow he had scraped acquaintance with Johnny Connor who staged a Battle Royal every week at the Empire Hotel, Springfield, Illinois, when twelve kids fought it out for a five-buck prize. He had carried the day in that shambles; and George Siler, the referee, had telegraphed a Chicago promoter that he'd just discovered a boy called Johnson, 'the greatest natural boxer I ever laid my eyes on.' This led to a ten-dollar purse for the bout against the fighter who was known as Must-Have-It Johnny, and when Jack won there were sodas for every member of the Avenue K gang of which he was the undisputed leader.

He told them the whole story, right up to the end—the bitter end. But as he told of them, defeat and eclipse didn't seem particularly bitter. They were just inevitable, as the turn of the tide down there in the Bay was inevitable; as the gleam and fading of the stars over the sea was inevitable. Another tide would roll in; the stars would shine again; another boy would be found, as once in the dockyards of Galveston, as once in the cottonfields of Alabama.

He came to an end. They cheered him and crowded round to touch his hand, to speak to him and to have him speak back to them.

'I knew your father, Jack. I remember you when you swept out the old school.'

'Say, Jack, how do you reckon good old Joe would go against McVey?'

'Listen, Jack, I got a kid, he works at the harbour, I bet he's got a punch Peter Jackson never got. You come and have a look at him, Jack.'

They gave him a last cheer as he left. He got into the car and waved good-bye. It was time to go back—he had an appointment in Samara.

XIX

◆◆◆

WHERE DOES HE STAND among the champions? Would he have beaten Sullivan—Corbett—Dempsey—Tunney—Marciano? What was his influence on boxing? Was he, the ring apart, a good citizen soured by ill luck, or a bad man to the marrow of his bones? One cannot leave Jack Johnson stranded on the beach of immortality without raising such queries as these.

As a boxer it has been claimed that he stands at the very top, perhaps in magnificent loneliness. His enemies attack him on two grounds. First, they say he was a great defensive boxer; secondly, they point out he fought very few fights indeed against really first-class men. The first argument is quite fallacious: the second has some truth in it.

The point about Johnson's defensive skill is that it was so marvellous and so rare that it was apt to obscure his much more commonplace gift of a punch. Early in his career George Gardner thought he had the heaviest punch in the business: so did Marvin Hart. Burns would never be just on the subject of Johnson's merits, but those who saw him up-ended by that historic right uppercut in the first round at Sydney had no doubt that Johnson could punch his weight. Jeffries (and Corbett in Jeffries' corner) knew that the Negro was one of the hardest hitters anyone had ever unleashed in the ring. Notice that even against Frank Moran, when he was out of condition and ageing, he had one chance of smashing home that right uppercut; and the blow broke Moran's nose in two places.

The chief evidence in support of Johnson's power as a puncher is contemporary, and it doesn't come from boxing circles at all, but from the common speech of the people. A heavy shell in World War I was nicknamed a 'Jack Johnson'. The world could have thought out no braver accolade than this spontaneous tribute.

Let us recapitulate his repertoire. Johnson's major punch was that formidable right uppercut, delivered after slipping his opponent's lead, bending forward with both feet balanced on the toes. But that long black serpent of a left lead was a masterpiece too. Yet neither of these tremendous blows hallmarked the champion. His speciality was the marvellous defensive punch that he shot home

178

against his adversary's biceps as he launched his own punch. It hurt more and tired out a man more than any other tactic in the game; and it was Johnson's trick, and uniquely Johnson's. Only he had the speed to launch it and land it while the other fellow's punch was on the way. One other speciality he had: the extraordinary gift of being able to lead to the jaw and re-slant the blow while it was on the way, so that it landed on the solar plexus. The switch came so swiftly and imperceptibly that it made defence almost an impossibility: nor did the blow lose in power from its change of direction.

Johnson was a magnificent in-fighter. Towering over Burns as he did and with much the longer arms, it would have been natural to expect him to try to keep that fighter at long range and to resist all the efforts of the little man to get in, capture the inside lines, and ram home short-arm jabs to the body at close-quarters. Yet Johnson was quite prepared to allow the fight to be fought on these lines. He was easily able to dominate Burns in that sort of campaign, despite Pat O'Keefe's belief that Burns was the greatest in-fighter in the world.

There remains a final point to be made to substantiate Johnson's claims to be a great puncher. The Negro was a lazy fellow and a lazy fighter. He was determined to inflict as much punishment as possible on Burns and Jeffries because they were his enemies, outside the ring as within. Against almost all other opponents, he was tolerant if not actually kindly. Observe the fate of two of these White Hopes: Al Kaufman and the superb middleweight Stan Ketchel.

Kaufman was a gigantic man with a mop of black hair and a handsome face. Johnson liked him, but he did not like the Californian crowd which soon began to crow: 'Go it, Al! Kill the nigger!' Johnson slipped Kaufman's attack and swung a right which he pulled up a couple of inches from the head. Then he turned to the crowd and shouted: 'You see what I can hand out? Now are you going to keep quiet?' The contest proceeded without benefit of advice from the hooligans; and Johnson finished far ahead on points. He could undoubtedly have knocked Kaufman out at any stage of the fight he chose. He didn't choose. He enjoyed Kaufman's company and was quite content to carry him till the bell.

He liked Stan Ketchel too, though he had no particular wish to box him, as he considered him too small to make a suitable opponent. Ketchel weighed, for this fight, 12 stone 2 pounds, some two stone less than the champion. He had taken part in fifty-eight contests,

forty-four of which he had won by knock-outs. There are many
fine judges who believe that, pound for pound, he was the greatest
fighter who ever graced the ring.

His battle with Johnson was a cross which became a double-
cross. Anxious to persuade more white heavyweights to give him a
chance to make money at their expense, Johnson agreed to allow
Ketchel to last out the contest. It wasn't an inspiring battle. Johnson's skilful defence and greater weight gave him the advantage,
but in the twelfth round Ketchel broke the agreement. He came in
with a wet sail, smashed down Johnson's guard and hurled over a
right hook designed to detach his man's head from his bull-neck.
The Negro sank in his tracks, and as he went down the crowd rose
up. The howls of delight ascended too. Surely the Negro was
beaten! Surely the white man had regained the ascendancy! The
howls redoubled as it was seen that Johnson was not finished with
yet. He was groping for the floor; he was up! Just as the crowd
started to shout: 'He's out!' he was up, and facing his man. Ketchel
came forward like a lion, springing in for the kill: he had double-
crossed his man, and got the chance of a lifetime. As he dashed up,
Johnson stood his ground, head bent slightly forward, and brought
up from the floor the most terrific uppercut of his career. Ketchel
went over as if shot through the brain and there was never the
slightest hope in any spectator's heart that he might beat the count.
When they took Johnson's gloves off a few minutes later they found
Ketchel's front teeth embedded in the right mitt.

Johnson had never been anxious to torture Ketchel as he tortured
Burns and Jeffries. He was quite content to allow Kaufman to coast
along for ten one-sided rounds. In the same year he allowed Victor
McLaglen, the film star, to remain perpendicular throughout a six-
round contest. He was content to lose most of the six rounds when
he fought O'Brien in Philadelphia, in the knowledge that no decision
could be given in that city to deprive him of his title. Unless provoked, he was lazy and good-natured in the ring; and this undoubtedly has lent colour to the rumour that he was not one of the
chief aggressive fighters in boxing's saga.

The other main argument against naming Johnson as the greatest
of the great has far more substance to it. His critics declare that he
fought few really first-class men; and to some extent they are right.
It should be pointed out, however, that when a man beats a whole
regiment of opponents, history has a way of dismissing the defeated
in one fell swoop as if they were pushovers. The long list of the

vanquished when Louis was king are thought of to-day as of no consequence whatever. But if Louis had not been on the scene, Billy Conn would have been acclaimed as a master; he would probably have made a worthier champion of the world than Sharkey or Carnera.

Johnson's case, however, was very different from Louis's. Joe fought all comers as champion: Jack held his title for seven years and met in that time only some two or three opponents of any stature whatever. If you judge Johnson as great (as I hope you do), it won't be because of his victories after he had won the title. His victories over Burns and Jeffries were, of course, the historic triumphs of his career, but Burns was a pigmy facing a giant, and Jeffries was far past his best. True, Johnson beat Ketchel consummately, but Ketchel was only a middleweight.

No—the great achievements in Jack's record were his victories over his Negro rivals: McVey, Langford, Jeannette. These were gained, it will be noticed, *before* Jack won his championship. He wasn't risking his title against the genuine challengers, who had, in the main, too few influential friends to make any fuss on their behalf. Who cared which Negro it was, if a Negro had to be champion of the world?

But though Johnson, having gained his place in the sun was unwilling to risk it, there could be no doubt that he was game to meet the best of them on his way to success. Notice how long he took to mature. Choynski knocked him out without much difficulty before he had any experience of opponents of the front rank, but he was of an age when most boxers are in their prime when Marvin Hart took from him a decision—admittedly a disputed decision. Many people who ought to know nominate Hart as about the least impressive name on the world championship roll. Johnson also lost on a foul to Jeannette in 1905: a result which suggests that he was certainly facing defeat in that contest. Experienced boxers, then as now, rarely committed fouls except to escape being more decisively beaten.

Well, there you are. Johnson beat the world's best and for seven years had really no rival in the ring. 'Peggy' Bettinson, who had no reason to love him, spoke of him as 'an immense pugilist'. Nat Fleischer, who has seen every champion from Johnson to Marciano, says in his fine book, *The Heavyweight Championship*: 'After years devoted to the study of heavyweight fighters, I have no hesitation in naming Jack Johnson as the greatest of them all.' He certainly dominated the landscape of boxing as only Joe Louis has dominated it since. Probably he would have beaten any of the other champions after his own day: but Tunney and Louis at his best must have been hard nuts for any man to crack.

Whatever may be one's own summing-up as to Johnson's place in the scheme of things, much interest appertains to the old master's view as to the merits of the men who succeeded him. He didn't, to be frank, think very much of them. Corbett was the prototype of the boxer as Johnson saw it; and next to Corbett came Peter Jackson. The hardest punchers he himself ever met were Hank Griffin and Choynski in his nonage and—when he was near his best—Bob Fitzsimmons, then forty-five years old. Of them all, he considered Fitzsimmons the supreme past-master among hitters. One colossal left, which didn't connect, Johnson vowed he heard as it passed him, humming like a swarm of bees.

To Braddock, Louis, Schmeling and Max Baer he paid few compliments. He was quite certain that they were inferior to Corbett, and even to Jeffries at his best. The best of them was, of course, Louis; but Johnson was reserved in his appreciation of the second Negro heavyweight champion of the world. He admitted that Louis was fast, and an accurate puncher. He acknowledged that he was skilful in defence and a quick thinker in the ring. What he did not like about Louis was his *stance*. He hadn't the balance of Corbett: he was too heavy-footed and rigid. Johnson was sure that Louis could be taken out of his stride by a hard-hitting fighter who thought fast and dazzled his man with a whole boxful of tricks. He was astute enough to predict that Schmeling would knock out the previously unbeaten Louis the first time they met. Louis was more generous to Johnson. He said simply on hearing of his death: 'He must have been a great fighter, as my trainer, Jack Blackburn, knew him well and said he was great.'

The best of his own successors Johnson named as Dempsey, whose vicious energy appealed to him. He liked Dempsey's terrific concentration on the job in hand, his speed and his instinctive gift for timing the delivery of the really important punches of a fight. But he faulted Dempsey too. The fire and fury that made him into a formidable opponent were concentrated into the first three or four rounds of a contest. After that Dempsey was just another good fighter; not a sabre-toothed tiger.

Probably Tunney with his coolness and his boxing skill would have given Johnson more trouble than any latterday champion, for the finest scientific boxer since Corbett was—as his battles with Greb prove—never averse to tangling with the most brutish customers in the ring on their own terms. Johnson admitted Tunney's cleverness but thought that the Old Guard (Corbett, Fitz or Jeffries) would have belted the daylight out of him.

Of all the men he had fought he thought McVey was the gamest. No other man ever took such punishment as Johnson handed out to Big Sam when he knocked him out with a mighty left hook in the twentieth round in 1904. McVey's face was a red pulp, his mouth was a great scarlet round and both his eyes were closed by the fifteenth round; yet his spirit was unbroken.

But though McVey was the bravest of them all, you couldn't, in Johnson's opinion, generalize about Negroes being tougher ring material, by divine right of nature, than white men. There were, according to him, no fighting races in the sense beloved by romantic sports writers. There were, however, certain races whose members had to fight or become submerged: these were the Irish, the Welsh, the Jews and the Negroes. If you were born into one of those races you were likely to develop any pugnacious instinct you might possess: if you were lucky enough to have been born uptown, you could go to your grave without ever revealing the superman within you. Such was Johnson's philosophical summing-up of the situation, though he did add as a foot-note that in his experience there were more white quitters than black in the ring.

After you have decided how Johnson rates among the major heavyweights since the days of the prize ring, the question still stands as to what sort of character the champion possessed. When we come to consider that question, the first points we must bear in mind are not concerned with the man himself, but with the background of his age and home. In America in Johnson's day, there was a colour bar that almost amounted to apartheid. No Negro would be tolerated in a hotel, theatre, church or even bus occupied by white Americans. In certain States it was illegal for a Negro to marry a white woman: in all States it was sternly forbidden by custom.

Among boxers it had been customary in the lighter weights for black to meet white; and men like Gans, Walcott and George Dixon, the best of their divisions, fought white men without a squeak of protest from the rest of the community. But there was always some special significance about the conduct of affairs in the heavyweight class. The welters and feathers belonged to that submerged tenth, the boxing community, who were no better than the fly-by-nights of the racing world; but the heavyweight division was a national institution, on all fours with Church and State. John L. Sullivan, who had raised the whole status of his trade by shaking hands with the Prince of Wales, had been the first to draw the colour bar. True, there were those who wondered whether this high-minded act had anything to do with his fears that Peter Jackson might be capable of knocking him head over heels. But what John L. said was gospel, and it became an understood thing that you could claim to be champion of the world without ever being called upon to face a Negro. Moreover, you didn't politely decline the honour. You called him a damn nigger, and you spat when you soiled your mouth by speaking his name.

Such was the background. What did Johnson do to change it? There was, it may be remarked, nothing to his discredit *before* he had become the best man in the world. As a young man he was a modest learner. Charles Brooks, the first to spot him in a Galveston gym, recommended him with confidence, as a man and a brother as well as a boxer, to Leo Posner of the Galveston Athletic Club. (If Brooks had any complaint to make it was that Posner picked on him to box a trial with Johnson, and the Negro repaid his kindness by knocking him senseless.)

It is probable that Posner had nothing to complain about in his relations with Johnson during the early part of the boxer's career. Nor, at first, had Sam Fitzpatrick, under whose management Johnson won his title. The fighter was well-behaved during his early years in the American ring. After he had beaten his three Negro rivals and Fitzsimmons and realized that he was the logical contender for a championship bout, he was still easy to control. He was a good boy at the National Sporting Club. He respectfully called Mr Bettinson 'sir'. He went to bed at ten o'clock: he was grateful to be allowed a seat on a bus.

Then came Australia, and victory over Burns, and the world championship. Immediately we behold a changed Johnson! The golden smile was half a golden snarl. The seat on the bus was exchanged for six motor-cars—no less—in an age when one was considered a luxury fit for a millionaire. The ladies and banquets which were almost orgies were given the champion's distinguished consideration. Worst of all, Sam Fitzpatrick, who had managed the great Peter Jackson, was tossed aside and all the promises he had made on Johnson's behalf were discarded as so many scraps of paper.

Johnson became quickly enough a marked man in his own country. Every white hand was against him: but weren't any of those hands raised in defiance before Johnson had offended? Remember Jack London's appeal to Jeffries—'The White Man must be rescued'. . . . Fighting words? In Jack London's defence must be stressed the fact that he had just been watching the white champion suffering the indignity of calculated humiliation and physical torture. In Johnson's defence it must be emphasized that Burns had done everything a man could, to provoke such punishment.

If Johnson was an ugly customer after he had beaten Burns, he became worse than ever when he rubbed in the lesson he now openly bragged he was teaching the white race, at the expense of Jeffries. The race riots that followed that contest cost eight lives. For Johnson the fight meant $120,000: most of which was spent in riotous living.

Then, when he was on top of the world, came the tragedies of Johnson's life. The first, the suicide of his first wife, was in his view entirely due to the persecution she had received as a race traitor, a white woman who had married the black who had been good enough to beat the best of whites in the ring. Possibly, however, his own gross and ruthless way of living contributed to Etta's determination to take her own life.

The death of his first white wife added greatly to Johnson's unpopularity in the States. His treatment of Belle Schreiber which entailed his trial under the Mann Act was the climax of his disgraceful career in American eyes. In exile he proved to be a slippery business man, and occasionally an ugly customer to deal with.

On balance, he may be described (in fact he generally *is* described) as the villain of the piece. He was a bad boy who failed to pay his rent, didn't always turn up to fulfil his contract, treated certain women shamefully, sometimes hit innocent citizens outside the ring. In a word, he seemed (as a promoted under-privileged person might seem) unable to hold his oats, for all these offences were committed, be it noted, during his hour of glory—he was a well-behaved citizen in the quarter of a century after he left Leavenworth Prison.

Suppose Jack Johnson had been born into a world in which race distinction didn't exist, in which a colour bar had never been raised? There is not a tittle of evidence to suggest that he would ever have gone off the rails. All his shortcomings, all his offences stem from the persecution he endured for years for the offence of possessing a black skin; and a successful black skin at that.

Will there ever be a world where the black man does not have to fight for his place in the sun? If the sun ever rises on such a world, will there be fighters among the black men—won't they, like the Jewish boys in the new Welfare State of Britain, be kept away by their families from the cruel trade, and given a chance to earn their living in a more humane and dignified manner? It is all too likely— but such a millennium is still far distant. You will still find your champions in the homes along the waterfront and the coal-face. You will still find that when they become champions they behave much as Tartar chiefs or invading armies are apt to behave.

If Johnson did harm to his calling and to his race, Joe Louis re-stored credit to both. He, too, had a hard row to hoe, but he was a man of more reflective temperament, though not (as I know, having discussed the problem with him) unaware of the impositions holding back the champion Negroes in his own and other countries. It was left to an American sports writer to give Louis his accolade: 'I am proud to be a member of his race—I mean, of course, the human race.' If anyone had ever talked to John Arthur Johnson in his for-mative years in such a vein, the whole history of boxing might have been a better and a brighter story.

Index